Endorsements

"When my friend Peter McHugh speaks, I try to listen. When he writes, I'm reading every word with care. After reading the manuscript twice, 'Radically Restored To Oneness with One Another' is a book that answers many of our prayers. Some books you read for information, some for inspiration; this one will lead to transformation. Jesus prayed for us to experience uncommon unity and a healthy community so that the world would believe (John 17:20-26). This book serves as a blueprint for establishing a culture of discipleship in the community, leading to a missional movement that will impact cities and nations with the kingdom of God. I highly recommend this book!"

Dr. Leif Hetland
Founder, Global Mission Awareness
Peachtree City, Georgia

"Peter and Lyn McHugh are two of the kindest and most hospitable people Rolland and I know. From the first moments we walked into their church and their home, we felt embraced and honored in a way that goes beyond words. Just their presence was like a warm hug! To us they are shining examples of what it means to seek and to live out the unity Jesus spoke about in John 17. Together we long to see the body of Christ standing united, one and whole. We know that in days to come Jesus will get all that He asked for. As you read Peter's powerful words, may you be brought into a deeper unity with the Lord and His beautiful body around the world."

Heidi G. Baker, Ph.D.
Co-founder and Executive Chairman of the Board, Iris Global
Pemba, Mozambique

"In the first book in this series, Peter McHugh explored the wonder of being radically restored to relationship with God. Now he explores the implications of that restoration to our relationships with one another. What are those implications? Peter will argue it's actually quite simple: just love one another as Christ has loved us. Problem is, that while it's a simple instruction to all who follow Jesus, it's not easy, and so much hangs on it. Jesus said that this was the key to the world knowing he had been sent by the Father. It's a simple instruction but it's not easy. How can there be oneness when you are so sure you are right and others are wrong? How can there be oneness when you are betrayed, criticised, misunderstood, treated unfairly, and confronted with ideas and perspectives with which you deeply disagree? In other words, how can we practise this part of our calling in Christ, to love each other as He loved us, while living together as imperfect and sometimes difficult people in a broken world? Allow Peter to lead you on a journey of discovery towards oneness with one another. A lot hangs on it."

Dr. Allan Meyer
Cofounder, Careforce Lifekeys
Melbourne, Australia

"It would be hard to imagine, in this season, that you could read a more important book than this one. Over recent years there has been, and continues to be, many wonderful books on the Great Commission, evangelism, discipleship, leadership, church planting etc., but hardly any on the only real means to actually achieve progress in the above important Christian topics, and that is the unity of the Body of Christ; Oneness, John 17 Oneness. Peter McHugh explores Oneness with an unapologetic use of scripture with profound and challenging exposition and application. A watching and waiting world needs to see Christian's in communities of Oneness to fully know and experience the love of the Father and Son. I commend this book to you."

Ian Shelton
Co-ordinator of Movement Australia
Toowoomba, Australia

"Having just been involved in a very painful situation, watching many suffer great pain and hurt, I have become absolutely committed to learning how I can improve the way I live in relationships and present the objective of a truly united bride. This book carries extraordinary yet applicable wisdom to that end. I commend this strategically timed manual to you for uniting the bride, walking in love and friendship and therefore fulfilling the desire of Jesus 'that we may be one'. It is nothing less than our Kingdom assignment and privilege".

Paul Manwaring
Itinerant teacher and organisational coach
Bethel Church Senior Leadership Team
Redding, California

"'Radically Restored to Oneness with One Another' is a poignant exploration of unity and reconciliation in our fractured world. With profound insights and practical wisdom, Pete invites readers to embrace the transformative power of forgiveness, empathy, and understanding. This book is a timely and inspiring call to build bridges, heal divisions, and foster genuine unity in our relationships and communities."

SHANE WILLARD
Shane Willard Ministries
Brisbane, Australia

"I am challenged, informed and inspired by Peter McHugh's second of four books. In my view, it addresses the most urgent and important issue facing the contemporary church. This book is the result of "the wedding of a brilliant and uncompromising mind with a heart that is warmly and wonderfully kind." My prayer is that a wide portion of Christian disciples, and especially Christian leaders, will be similarly challenged, informed and inspired."

DR. KEITH FARMER
Mentor
Principal, Emeritus Australian College of Ministries
Central Coast, Australia

FOREWORDS BY BILL JOHNSON
& GRAHAM COOKE

RADICALLY RESTORED

TO ONENESS WITH ONE ANOTHER

Embracing Jesus' Kingdom Perspective

PETER McHUGH

© 2024 The Hanerda Trust

All rights reserved Apart from any fair dealing for the purposed of private study, research, criticism or review, as permitted under the Copyright Act, no part may be reproduced by any process without written permission.

Unless otherwise stated Scripture taken from the NEW AMERICAN STANDARD BIBLE®, Copyright © 1960, 1962, 1963, 1971, 1972, 1975, 1977, 1995 bynthe Lockman Foundation. Used by permission.

All enquiries regarding this publication and Peter McHugh's speaking engagements should be directed to:

Stairway Church Whitehorse
171 Rooks Road, Vermont, Vic

PO Box, 3092, Nunawading BC, Vic 3131

Telephone: +61 3 9837 2900

Email: peter.mchugh@stairway.org.au

Sourced from Amazon and Ingram Spark.
Cover and book design by Ilana McMorran

ISBN 978-1-7636182-3-7

Acknowledgements

I count it as one of the greatest privileges of my life to have served the Stairway Church community for over 30 years. From the time Lyn (my wife) and I planted the church in February 1990, our walk with God has been empowered through this wonderful congregation. They have loved us, believed in us, and carried us through some very challenging moments. The content found in the Radically Restored series of books has been discovered and fashioned in this context. Thank you, Stairway.

The Lord's favour on Stairway has opened the doors through which many friendships beyond Stairway have been established. These friendships have significantly impacted the way I both see my relationship with God and walk with Him. In particular, I will remain forever thankful for Bill Johnson, Graham Cooke, David Wagner, Leif Hetland and Allan Meyer as they have released so much to me.

I write all my books by hand. That is, I pick up a pen and hand-write the first draft onto paper. This second book in the Radically Restored series was typed from my handwritten draft by Paula Taylor (my long-term personal assistant) and Hannah Easton (my long-loving eldest daughter). Thank you Paula and Hannah for your tireless efforts in interpreting my handwriting and your countless suggested improvements to the way I express my thoughts.

My thanks to Edwina Vance who kindly read the early manuscript and offered very helpful feedback. Edwina encouraged some additional creative ways to both express and clarify my thoughts.

My deepest thanks go to Lyn. Our life together, the family we have raised, and the nine grandchildren we are doing our best to spoil mean more to me than words can adequately express. Lyn's love, deep conversations, shared ups and downs, and prayers are the bedrock upon which I build.

Finally and of course, the Lord—my Father God, my brother Jesus, and my instructor Holy Spirit—have made these pages possible. Thank you for trusting me with Your Word and insights. They have not just changed my life, but I have observed the profound changes in tens of thousands of people through Your encounters with them.

Contents

Foreword from Bill Johnson 1

Foreword from Graham Cooke 3

Important Note 7

Preface 9

Introduction 17

Chapter 1
The Call to Love Others 35

Chapter 2
A Call to Kingdom Relational Values 63

Chapter 3
A Call to Practice with Diligence 99

Chapter 4
A Call to Transformation 135

Chapter 5
A Call to Action 169

Concluding Words
Stay the Course 187

Biography 191

Foreword from
Bill Johnson

If this book were written by a stranger, I would celebrate it and encourage you to prioritize the time needed to read it. It's that good. But knowing that it was written by Peter McHugh, who is not only a dear friend but also one of the most trusted leaders I know, I especially recommend it. I greatly admire him, as he is so intentional in everything he does. He uncompromisingly focuses on all that is right and does so with wisdom and grace. You never feel intimidated when you're around him. Instead, you feel inspired. We need more like him. Many more like him.

The Church is meant to be a beacon of hope for a world that is searching for answers. But we can only be that when we come together. Our unity is what will enable us to more fully display the reality of who Jesus is. In an orchestra, it's possible for the instruments to be in tune with each other yet be out of tune because they have adjusted to the wrong pitch. To prevent that, the conductor takes a tuning fork, which produces the correct sound. All the instruments then tune themselves to that one sound. All the instruments become united by tuning themselves to one standard; thus, by design, they find themselves in tune with each other. Unity with one another within the Church begins by being united with and surrendered to Him.

In my annual trips to Stairway Church in Australia, I have been deeply marked by the highly evident value for people that both Peter and his wife, Lyn, model for the rest of us. For them, unity and oneness are not simply terms that are in vogue. The heart of the Lord Jesus, as seen in John 17, has become their heart. They are moved by what has moved Him.

And in John 17, Jesus gives us that powerful, priestly prayer. He concludes with a statement that is difficult to fully comprehend: "that they all may be one, as You, Father, are in Me, and I in You…" (v. 20). This is a gut-level cry of Jesus. In these final moments before the crucifixion, He is asking His Father to do something in you and me that has only existed in the Godhead. It's as if Jesus is praying for the supernatural dimension of love and affection that the Father, Son, and Holy Spirit enjoy together, to become the normal experience for every believer—now and in this life. His prayers are always answered. And may this one be answered in our lifetime.

True, biblical unity requires diversity. Unity without diversity is uniformity. There's a unique expression seen through every gift, every talent, and through our individual histories. All those things are to be celebrated and protected. Of course, Jesus' value for unity doesn't mean that we compromise our beliefs or values, but it does mean that our love must be greater than our ability to be offended. We know that "love covers a multitude of sins" (1 Peter 4:8).

We have an invitation to model true unity to the world around us in such a way that many are drawn to the Lord, as in the book of Acts. Radically Restored…to Oneness with One Another is a wonderful resource to help us do that well. It's filled with practical insights for building strong relationships and a clear biblical call for us to become the answer to Jesus' prayer. This begins with you and me. May we be ones who are known by the way we love, demonstrating who He is and bringing the reality of heaven to earth.

BILL JOHNSON
Senior Leader of Bethel Church, Redding, CA
Author of Born for Significance and Hosting the Presence

Foreword from
Graham Cooke

I have decided to write this foreword not just as a friend of Peter, whose leadership values I champion, but also as a prophet, one mindful of the will of God.

I have known Peter as a close and personal friend for several decades and more. I have watched him grow and change because God pursued him, and Peter made time to become caught up in the Father's embrace.

Our mutual conversations with our wives Lyn and my Teresa, have been joyful, fruitful, and eye opening. We always stayed in their home, where children and grandchildren came to visit, bringing life, love and laughter that seem to make the house bigger.

Early morning conversations with Peter created a real buzz, in my heart and affection with the Lord. Our friendship together became a shared space with the Father.

Jesus is always a magnet for love with kindness. He can never be outdone in sharing the beauty of the Godhead in close and loving intimacy. To know and be loved by Jesus is to experience the fullness of Love available in Kingdom Life. On Earth as it is in Heaven.

Sadly much of this unparalleled beauty has been lost to the tyranny of religious practices that do not make necessary space available for the true adoration of God in divine fellowship.

Full access to God's beauty is of paramount importance in our growth and discipleship in the Kingdom. On Earth as it is in Heaven, is the only means to experience the fullness of God in Christ, in our heart and mind.

We spend more time on people's unreality of God's presence than we do on empowering their growth in His goodness and loving kindness. God is the kindest person I have ever known!

When did the church become less mindful of God's love? Why did we assume that everyone was accessing the fullness of God's love just because we taught it as a bible study?

Only practice makes something permanent!

I love the whole seed analogy that Jesus spoke of in the gospels. Because of Jesus being the sower of seeds into our hearts there is no shortage of fruit bearing potential in our lives.

Part of the real connection of Agape love in our hearts is that Jesus is both sower and reaper. It is He who cultivates enrichment in our life circumstances.

The Presence of God acts as a nutrient to the soil in our hearts. His health overflows in a multiplicity of ways. He abounds towards us in all things. Abundance is His life, promised to us so that we would abound in all things.

A good starting place to learn how to abound is:

> *"God is able to make all grace abound to you, so that always having all sufficiency in everything, you may have an abundance for every good deed."*
>
> 2 Cor 9:8
>
> *"And this I pray, that your love may abound still more and more, in real knowledge and all the discernment. So that you may approve the things that are excellent, in order to be sincere and blameless until the day of Christ."*
>
> Phil.1:9-10.
>
> *"...and may the Lord cause you to increase and abound in love for one another, and for all people just as we also do for you; so that He may establish your hearts without blame in holiness before our God and Father at the coming of our Lord Jesus Christ."*
>
> 1 Thess 3:12-13

The only thing that prevents abundance from becoming a real power in our lives is the lack of focused loving in our hearts.

In spiritual terms, the church is defined by the degradation, the sinfulness, the unremitting sadness of poverty and sickness and the corruption of people in places of power in our communities. The sheer numbers of people suffering in our city is testimony of our powerlessness as the Body of Christ.

Where is the Oneness in Unity with Father, Son and Spirit?

Why are we so divided into factions?

FOREWORD

Why is the enemy winning all around us?

It is the lack of fullness of love for God that can only be created by the overwhelming love of His Presence in us and in one another.

This book has the call of God in its language. There are no shades of grey here. It's black and white! We care for what God wants or we ignore him.

We position ourselves for real purposeful change, or we do not.

We exemplify the agenda of the Redeemer, or we deny him.

We love the lost, the despised, and their suffering around us, or we refuse to help people.

We have a divided Church with poor relational values because the deceiver is present.

There is no middle ground.

Only in the covenant community of love, where we are practising being of one heart and mind with God and one another, can we become the image bearers of Christ in the place where we live.

Jesus did not come that we might have meetings and have them more abundantly. He came, that we would know His true abundance, because of His fullness of presence in us.

I love this book as I love this author. It is full of God's love, grace, kindness and truth.

Most churches are not a community in real terms, just a meeting place for themselves.

We grow by what we receive and we give by what God grows in us by abundance. A church that does not practice love as God defines it cannot be trusted. Such a group of people will have a hard time on 'that day' in heaven.

Love is not an option, it is a necessity. If you really want to grow up into all things in Christ, you must at least begin by studying and practising the one another's in Scripture.

In your congregation, if God's love is not a ruling power, then you are not living in God's image and likeness. Genesis 1:26 is governed by the Law of First mention. When God says something for the first time He sets a precedent and by that precedent He can be known forever!

Lack of first love means that your spirituality is suspect. It has been tainted by other things being more valuable to us in our community.

In Christ we exemplify Heaven on Earth as a lifestyle. This is how we know the truth from the false. This is how we prove His Lordship in our midst.

The early church were the forerunners of change; people who turned the world upside down. The modern Church acts as a refuge from change.

Everything in this book is both a message and a pointer towards working with God to His satisfaction. At the very least read Isaiah chapter 53 concerning the suffering servant, who is Jesus.

Regarding the quality of your church, can He look back on the anguish of His soul and be satisfied with who you are in him?

If that question cannot be answered in all honesty, I suggest that you read Matthew chapter 25. God grant beloved, that at the very least, you will have the grace to start weeping.

GRAHAM COOKE
Brilliant Perspectives, International Author and Speaker

Important Note
TO BE READ CAREFULLY

Why do I quote and re-present in full so much of the Word in what I have written?*

There are two reasons.

The first is that the Barna Research Group, regarding religion in 2009, made the following observations:

'Most self-identified Christians are comfortable with the idea that the Bible and the sacred books from non-Christian religions all teach the same truth and principles.'

'Bible reading has become the religious equivalent of sound-bite journalism. When people read from the Bible, they typically open it, read a brief passage without much regard for the context, and consider the primary thought or feeling that the passage provided. If they are comfortable with it, they accept it; otherwise, they deem it interesting but irrelevant to their life and move on. There is shockingly little growth evident in people's understanding of the fundamental themes of the scriptures and amazingly little interest in deepening their knowledge and application of biblical principles.'[1]

The second is that Mark 4: 1 – 12, Matthew 13: 1 – 15, and Luke 8: 4 – 10, Jesus tells the parable of the sower and the seed. The disciples could not understand what they were hearing and asked for an explanation. Jesus begins His explanation by telling His disciples that in this parable, they have been given the mystery or key to the Kingdom of God.

The mystery or key is that all spiritual truth and subsequent insight and revelation comes in the form of a seed, and that seed is the word of God.

As I came to write these four books, I was aware of the Holy Spirit imploring me to, as much as possible, not just give reference to the word of God but to actually quote it for all to read. I am convinced that our journey of discipleship, transformation, and spiritual maturity is enhanced, empowered, and

---

1 Important Note
* Unless specified otherwise, all scripture references are taken from the New American Standard Bible
 BARNA GROUP (2009), Barna Studies the Research, Offers a Year-in-Review Perspective Retrieved from https://www.barna.com/research/barna-studies-the-research-offers-a-year-in-review-perspective/ on September 6th 2021

accelerated when the Spirit and Word come together in a moment of insight that takes root in our heart and grows through its application.

Without the seed of God's word, our spiritual lives wither away, and our capacity to represent Jesus well is limited. Deuteronomy 8: 3 declares an eternal perspective of our need for the Word:

> *He humbled you and let you be hungry, and fed you with manna which you did not know, nor did your fathers know, that He might make you understand that man does not live by bread alone, but man lives by everything that proceeds out of the mouth of the Lord.*

Equally, the other essential ingredient to the seed, the Word, is the soil or heart posture and condition of the one reading and receiving the Word. Jesus, when speaking to those who had believed Him yet were seeking to kill Him, observes in John 8: 37 that this was the case for one reason: 'because My word makes no progress in you.' The seed carries the same potential to change a life and the world around them to everyone who hears. Yet that potential is only released fully through those who have humble and meek hearts who want to fully surrender to the Lordship of Jesus.

My strongest encouragement to you as you come to this book is to purposefully read the quoted word of God through a prayerfully surrendered heart that longs to live a life of receiving, becoming, and releasing the love of God.

Preface

Have you ever driven in Italy?

I have found it quite an experience after driving in Australia for 45 years.

The apparent overarching philosophy of drivers in Italy is an aggressive mindset of everyone for themselves where you don't give an inch. This mindset then translates into several behaviours or practices:

— Hesitation means you are not going;

— The left lane is ONLY for passing at high speeds;

— Stop signs don't mean stop; instead, they mean make sure the coast is clear before proceeding;

— Horns are a mode of communication, not anger;

— Drive aggressively to fit into the gap they see ahead as they do not care about what is going on behind them; and,

— When changing lanes, blinkers say, here I go, not I want to go, or I'm waiting to see if you will let me go.

When I first started driving in Italy, I was completely unaware of these practices and consequently had very little idea of what was going on or why people were making certain choices. However, after the first week, I became familiar with this new mindset; it began to make sense, and I strangely appreciated it!

Much like I had to become accustomed to a new set of driving practices to drive like the people of Italy and 'be one' with that culture, across the body of Christ, there is a rising prophetic voice calling God's people to become familiar with and adopt Kingdom practices. Practices that will enable us to be an answer to Jesus' prayer in John 17:20-22:

> "I do not ask on behalf of these alone, but for those also who believe in Me through their word; that they may all be one; even as You, Father, are in Me and I in You, that they also may be in Us, so that the world may believe that You sent Me. The glory which You have given Me I have given to them, that they may be one, just as We are one; I in them and You in Me, that they may be perfected in unity, so that the world may know that You sent Me, and loved them, even as You have loved Me."

Greg Boyd, in his book 'Repenting of Religion', writes:

> We must confess that Jesus' prayer for the church to manifest the perfect, loving unity of the triune God has by and large not been fulfilled. Whatever else the church may be known for in the world, it is not generally known for exemplifying a distinctive, radical, self-sacrificial love, either toward those within the body of Christ or toward those without. The church generally has not left people with the impression that we are unique in the way we affirm the unsurpassable worth of each individual regardless of how immoral and unlovable they may be.
>
> If anything, the church today is largely known for its petty divisiveness along denominational, doctrinal, social, and even racial lines. On the whole, it is perceived as being *less* loving and *less* accepting than most other communities. It is often known for its self-proclaimed and often hypocritical alliance with good against evil and for its judgmentalism toward those it concludes are *evil*. But, tragically, as a corporate body it rarely is known as being distinctive because of its radical love. In contrast to Jesus' prayer, the world is *not* compelled to believe in the triune God on the grounds that his love is undeniably present among Jesus' disciples.[2]

Similarly, Andy Stanley, in his book 'Irresistible' writes:

> ...Imagine a world where people were skeptical of what we believed but envious of how well we treated one another...Once upon a time it was so. Once upon a time the *one-another* culture of the church stood in sharp contrast to the "bite and devour" one-another culture of the pagan world.... Paul's *one-another* list should epitomise the reputation of those who call themselves Christians. When people outside the church think about folks inside the church, the items on Paul's list should come to mind.... After all, Paul said, "the only thing that counts is faith expressing itself through love."[3]

I felt the Lord call me to add my voice to the growing chorus of voices very clearly in March 2018 on a trip between Melbourne, Australia, and Adelaide, Australia.

---

[2] Greg Boyd, Repenting of Religion: Turning from Judgment to the Love of God (Baker Books, 2004), Ch2 – Conclusion (accessed via eBooks therefore page number is not provided)
[3] Andy Stanley, Irresistible: Reclaiming the New That Jesus Unleashed for the World. (Zondervan, 2020) pg 216 – 217

PREFACE

I have had the privilege of traveling a great deal over the last 25 years, and there are some things that you get used to simply not happening as much as you'd like them to! When we arrived in Adelaide, we went to collect our bag from the carousel and found our bag was the first to come off the plane. This is one of those 'it just doesn't happen' things!! It had never happened before, nor has it happened since! Its unusualness caused me to lean into Holy Spirit, and I felt His prompting me; take note, this event is significant.

We went from the airport to our accommodation at a beachside set of apartments. There were six units, and we were in Apartment One. Again, the Holy Spirit prompted me to take note that there was something significant to this 'apartment one'. The Lord had my attention! I was curious and intrigued by what He might be trying to show me through the number "one".

As I pondered with the Lord over the few hours between our arrival and dinner, I became convinced that we would be seated at Table One at dinner that night. I spoke to Lyn, my wife, about what I was observing and sensing, including my belief that we'd be seated at Table One. We arrived at our dinner venue with our hosts, who knew nothing of what was happening, and surprise! We were shown to Table One.

For me, three occurrences were well and truly enough to get my attention! However, the Lord then shows off and makes His point abundantly clear. When we returned to Melbourne, the monitors showed that our flight's luggage would be at carousel number two. We were waiting at carousel two for our bags with all the other passengers from our flight. Another passenger collected their bag, and as the standing area was very small, I turned to make sure they had enough room to pass behind me. As I turned, I saw one bag, on Carousel Number One, with no passengers waiting there, and it was my bag!

In the months leading up to this ministry trip to Adelaide, I had been on a journey with the Lord in my devotional life. He was unpacking thoughts with me about reconciled diversity being a key to how God's people could be an answer to Jesus' prayer in John 17: 20 – 23. All these events during the trip to Adelaide strongly affirmed that He was asking me to carry this message of oneness, that is, reconciled diversity wherever I could. As a result, this four-book series RADICALLY RESTORED has come to life.

The term 'reconciled diversity' means that we reconcile within ourselves that expressions of the Kingdom of God through the many denominations, movements, and networks are not to be seen as requiring change or adjustment. We all need relationships for 'identity'. There were twelve tribes in the nation of Israel, each with a particular role to play and land to occupy. Each tribe was not focused on changing the other tribes, asserting that their tribe was right and the others wrong, nor making it clear that their tribe was better than the others. They acknowledged diversity as being what it was.

For followers of Jesus to be an answer to Jesus' prayer of being one requires a heart posture of being reconciled to the fact that we will not agree on everything. While we agree on ninety-five percent of theological questions, we are called to agree to disagree about the remaining five percent. We need to avoid striving to prove who is right and who is wrong. Equally, the ways we practice our faith are diverse, and we are called to honor and respect the traditions and ways of prayer and worship found across the Body of Christ. As we adopt the perspective of reconciled diversity, we begin to look to relationships for 'impact'. Jesus declared our oneness would result in the world knowing the Father had sent the Son.

When we put our trust in Jesus, when we are born again, we are radically restored into oneness with God (John 17: 21). Jesus promised that when we placed our faith in Him through repentance, the Godhead would make their abode in us. We would no longer be orphans (John 14: 18). Paul understands this as a mystery, "which is Christ in you, the hope of glory" (Col. 1: 27). Paul describes this radical restoration as "receiving the adoption as sons" (Gal. 4: 4 – 7).

Understandably the profound nature of this restoration has significant implications for how we live out our personal spirituality and journey (Rom.8: 29; 1 John 4: 15 – 17). To help us understand this significance, Jesus rewrote the second of the two great commandments of the Old Testament. He moved from "love one another as you love yourself" to: "love one another, *as I have loved you.*" In so doing, He expects us (it is a command) to know in our hearts, through experience and encounter, the love God has for us. This new command surpasses the more familiar experiences of knowing something intellectually (Eph. 3: 19). This knowledge was so profoundly significant to Paul in establishing the church that he wrote:

> *But the goal of our instruction is love from a pure heart and a good conscience, and a sincere faith.*
>
> 1 Tim. 1 – 5

Jesus makes it clear that the radical restoration of being one with God needs to flow into a radical restoration of being one with one another. The outcome of these radical restorations is societal transformation. That is, "the world may believe that You sent Me" (John 17:20– 21).

The apostle Peter recognized the significance of understanding that being radically restored to oneness with God should result in our pursuit of being radically restored to oneness with one another. In 2 Peter 1:5, he writes: 'Now for this very reason also, applying…' In verses two to four, Peter describes how we have become one with God and can now live in oneness with God by 'becoming partakers of the divine nature.' For this reason, we are to apply ourselves to a lifestyle that ultimately results in brotherly kindness and love, that is, oneness with others.

Peter then stresses the absolute centrality of building our spirituality on oneness with God and one another when he declares:

> *For if these **qualities** are yours and are increasing, they render you neither useless nor unfruitful in the true knowledge of our Lord Jesus Christ. For he who lacks these **qualities** is blind **or** short-sighted, having forgotten **his** purification from his former sins.*
>
> 2 Pet. 1: 8 – 9

It then appears that he is not content that he has adequately explained the significance of following Jesus through a focus on oneness with God and others and so then goes on to write:

> *Therefore, brethren, be all the more diligent to make certain about His calling and choosing you; for as long as you practice these things, you will never stumble; for in this way the entrance into the eternal kingdom of our Lord and Savior Jesus Christ will be abundantly supplied to you.*
>
> 2 Pet.1: 10 – 11

Finally, he sees it as a privilege and necessity to remind them of the need to live this way from oneness with God and others. Even when he has passed away, they would call this teaching to mind.

> *Therefore, I will always be ready to remind you of these things, even though you already know them, and have been established in the truth which is present with you. I consider it right, as long as I am in this earthly dwelling, to stir you up by way of reminder, knowing that the laying aside of my earthly dwelling is imminent, as also our Lord Jesus Christ*

has made clear to me. And I will also be diligent that at any time after my departure you will be able to call these things to mind.

2 Pet. 1: 12 – 15

Like Greg Boyd and Andy Stanley, when I was leading Stairway (I handed the leadership over in February 2023) we reexamined how as a community we would live together as God's people. With the governance teams of Stairway, we have identified the need to become a different sort of 'driver' of the vehicle called the church. To no longer drive with the practices associated with the church being an end in itself but rather to learn to drive with the practices related to the church being a means to the coming of the Kingdom. (See Diagram 1)

WHY DOES ANY CHURCH EXIST?

Church as an end in itself		Church as a means to the coming of the Kingdom
to growth ◀	**KEYS**	▶ to Kingdom
based on achievement ◀	**VALUES**	▶ based in Who we reveal
of the church ◀	**DISCIPLES**	▶ who learn to walk wit God
servant ◀	**IDENTITY**	▶ son/daughter
develop & manage programmes ◀	**LEADERS**	▶ empower spiritual growth
gifts/skills/ability/practices/ activity-led ◀	**LEADERS FOCUS**	▶ personal spirituality life/ presence/oneness
functional relationships to grow church numbers ◀	**WINESKIN**	▶ personal relationships that grow people who advance the Kingdom
telling for the purpose of agreement ◀	**COMMUNICATION STYLE**	▶ understanding for the purpose of knowing and being known
provision ◀ functional (tasks) circumstantial role & position principles (outcomes) shoulder to shoulder	**SPIRITUAL FOCUS**	▶ promises relational (honour) spiritual struggles & triumphs presence (heart transformation) heart to heart
seating capacity ◀	**SUNDAY**	▶ sending capacity (assignments)
earth to heaven unity of purpose ◀	**PRAYER**	▶ heaven to earth unity of heart

Diagram 1

PREFACE

The four-book series, RADICALLY RESTORED, is written to help the reader on their journey of being a disciple of Jesus who sees the Kingdom coming through their lives.

Book One
RADICALLY RESTORED…*to oneness with God*

Book Two
RADICALLY RESTORED…*to oneness with one another*

Book Three
RADICALLY RESTORED…*to release oneness for societal transformation*

Book Four
RADICALLY RESTORED…*leadership practices for establishing a culture of oneness*

I welcome you to a journey based on curiosity and discovery with a view to a reformation for God's people and His church.

Introduction

- The Lord is one - living in a covenant community of love.

- As His image bearers, we are to practice the qualities that lead us to live in oneness with one another.

- Being members of one another.

- Placing oneness with God and others as our highest value.

In October of 2004, life felt particularly good. Lyn and I had been following Jesus for over 22 years and leading Stairway Church for nearly 15 years since founding it and had weathered some rather traumatic times. Stairway was growing in national influence in Australia and developing some international relationships and influence.

In this context, I was a little surprised to find the Holy Spirit whispering to me in my devotional life, leading me to consider areas of my life where I might have allowed myself to be influenced by fear. As I allowed Him to speak and reveal things to me, I began to see that four specific fears had indeed impacted my heart and life: a fear of failure, a fear of rejection, a fear of being taken advantage of, and a fear of being misunderstood.

As each day passed in November 2004, I was increasingly confronted by the depth and breadth of these fears and how they had distorted my perception and impacted my behaviour. The distortion and impact were particularly evident when I was feeling under pressure, especially the stress of relational tension or circumstantial turmoil. In these situations, I was confronted by a sense of needing to 'fix' or 'be in control' of something that was not as it should be. It was becoming increasingly evident that I was a source of tension and pressure for others. I was beginning to recognize that my fear led me to respond in ways that were self-serving, self-centred, and self-reliant.

By December of 2004, I was overwhelmed with uncertainty that I could continue to offer leadership to Stairway. I was somewhat consumed with grief following the recognition that I was stuck in not-so-great practices in how I loved others, including how I provided, or more accurately *didn't* provide, a place of security for them. It was a most distressing place to find myself in. And much to my dismay, there was no clear path through the darkness I was engulfed by.

Knowing I couldn't find my way through alone, in January 2005, I reached out to some trusted friends who directed me to some spiritual formation literature. I found what I was experiencing was not a new phenomenon. I was accurately mirroring the story of the lives of countless other followers of Jesus down through the centuries. It was then I realized Holy Spirit was leading me to see the reality and impact of these fears because He wanted to counsel me into a place of freedom.

I knew *intellectually* the bible taught that 'perfect love casts out all fear' (1 John 4:18). The actual presence of these four fears revealed to me that I lacked the depth in my *experience* of the love of God that was needed to overcome them. I had allowed the roots of these four fears in my life to grow deep. I thought that they would protect the image I had created for myself, albeit a false one, to gain the acceptance of other people.[4]

Ephesians 3: 19 says:

> *and to know the love of Christ which surpasses knowledge, that you may be filled up to all the fullness of God.*

The Greek word here for 'know' means: 'to know by experience and encounter.' That is, to have heart knowledge. Paul is declaring that 'heart knowledge' of God's love for, and affection towards us, needs to surpass 'head knowledge' if we are to be filled up to the fullness of God.

Towards the end of January 2005, I knew the Holy Spirit was inviting me to allow Him to reveal where my roots of fear had developed. I embarked upon a discovery process of self-awareness and personal responsibility where I confronted the lies of my self-talk and internal conversations that had amplified the voices of fear above the voice of God's love and acceptance.

This journey of discovery helped me to see that to move forward, I needed to confront the lies of my 'inner truth'—lies that contradicted the truth of God's Kingdom and His worldview. As I let go of things that were so familiar and had created a strong sense of security, regardless of it being false, it was a disorientating and tortuous time in my life. I descended into increasingly deeper places of despair and hopelessness.

Feeling stuck and in need of some clear space and a fresh perspective, I travelled to visit some close friends in Auckland, New Zealand, in June of 2005. During this trip, I had a profound, life-changing encounter and experience with the love of God. This moment in my history with God changed everything…literally everything!

I returned home changed and have since walked in relationship with God based on a totally different foundation. A foundation of acceptance rather than performance.

RADICALLY RESTORED TO ONENESS WITH GOD

The book you hold in your hands now is the second in a series of four. In this book, I intend to build on the insights I share in, 'Radically Restored to One-

---

[4] In my book, Radically Restored…to oneness with God, I describe the process we engage with in the creation of our own identity. In my book, A Voyage of Mercy, I chronicle the details of my experience how the Lord set me free from these four fears.

ness with God'. So that we are starting on the same page, for those who have not read Book One, here is a brief overview:

— We need to become familiar with the practices required to be an answer to Jesus' prayer in John 17. That we would be one even as God is one; that is, we learn to live in reconciled diversity.

— As we seek out the answer to the age-old question 'who am I?' we each craft an answer and build an identity that helps us feel that we belong, are significant, and can be secure. This creates an outcome of finding identity in our performance. However, identity as a follower of Jesus is found in His love for and acceptance of us.

— The first Adam exchanged oneness with God for being like God in having the ability to make judgments. He (the first Adam) exchanged fathers, from God to Satan, and elevated the expression of our lordship. The second Adam, Jesus, restored oneness and relationship with God as Father. He replaced the reliance on judgment with the pursuit of compassion. Now, He establishes His kingdom on earth through followers who know who they are in Christ.

— Jesus rewrote the second of the two great commandments of the Old Testament. He instituted a greater commandment of 'love one another as I have loved you'. We are to make disciples who 'guard from loss by keeping their eye upon' how much they are loved by God. Now, we can love others from knowing how deeply we are loved.

— The Law is no longer there to describe and assess righteousness. It is not the source of our righteousness, but it is forever the course of our righteousness. Therefore, our spirituality and maturity are not to be measured by how well we follow the rules. Instead, it is measured by our transformation as a disciple of Jesus as we are committed to living more and more like Him every day.

— Jesus invites us to keep company with Him, living as much loved children and learning to live freely and lightly. This style of relational learning has grasped the reality of being chosen, holy and beloved. From this perspective, we are to consider our old ways as no longer having power over us. We are to change what we believe. To learn through transformation and being renewed by the Spirit and the Word how to put off behaviour that does not reflect the image of Jesus.

INTRODUCTION

— Grace is the empowering presence of God. It is the strength God gives us to live from the inheritance of being in Christ, being like Jesus in every circumstance through life. If our understanding of God is still informed by His judgement of our behaviour, this will lead us away from relying on His great grace and learning to live from what we've received.

Having looked in depth at the vertical relationship between God and ourselves in Book One, in this book, we'll explore how oneness is expressed in the horizontal relationships in life; the 'one anothers'.

ECHAD: THE LORD IS ONE

Hear, O Israel! The Lord is our God, the Lord is one! You shall love the Lord your God with all your heart and with all your soul and with all your might. These words, which I am commanding you today, shall be on your heart. You shall teach them diligently to your sons and shall talk of them when you sit in your house and when you walk by the way and when you lie down and when you rise up. You shall bind them as a sign on your hand and they shall be as frontals on your forehead. You shall write them on the doorposts of your house and on your gates.

Deuteronomy 6:4-9

'The Lord is one.' The Hebrew word for 'one' is *echad*. God is trinitarian. Three persons in one. God's oneness is expressed through being a covenant community of love. Their oneness is displayed through 'unity in diversity.'

Their attribute of oneness is manifest through all creation.

For from Him and through Him and to Him are all things. To Him be the glory forever. Amen.

Romans 11:36

...one God and Father of all who is over all and through all and in all.

Ephesians 4:6

Therefore, I was angry with this generation and said, 'they always go astray in their heart, and they did not know my ways';

Hebrews 3:10

We are created to exist in oneness with God.

> *...yet for us there is but one God, the Father, from whom are all things and we exist for Him; and one Lord, Jesus Christ, by whom are all things, and we exist through Him.*
>
> 1 Corinthians 8:6

Equally, their love first created us and now restores us to live in oneness with God.

> *...to whom God willed to make known what is the riches of the glory of this mystery among the Gentiles, which is Christ in you, the hope of glory.*
>
> Colossians 1:27

> *Therefore if you have been raised up with Christ, keep seeking the things above, where Christ is, seated at the right hand of God. Set your mind on the things above, not on the things that are on earth. For you have died and your life is hidden with Christ in God. When Christ, who is our life, is revealed, then you also will be revealed with Him in glory.*
>
> Colossians 3:1-4

The centrality and significance of oneness to who God is and how they live together is to be illustrated in marriage.

> *For this reason, a man shall leave his Father and his mother, and be joined to his wife; and they shall become one flesh.*
>
> Genesis 2:24

To become one (*echad*) flesh is to demonstrate the nature of God. God's idea of marriage is that it would reveal who He is and show God's likeness. God hates divorce because it violates the essence of oneness, that which holds everything together.

Therefore, anything that sabotages *echad*, oneness, is to be avoided and put off.

> *But now you also, put them all aside: anger, wrath, malice, slander,* **and** *abusive speech from your mouth.*
>
> Colossians 3:8

INTRODUCTION

> *Now the deeds of the flesh are evident, which are: immorality, impurity, sensuality, idolatry, sorcery, enmities, strife, jealously, outbursts of anger, disputes, dissensions, factions, envying, drunkenness, carousing, and things like these, of which I forewarn you, just as I have forewarned you, that those who practice such things will not inherit the kingdom of God.*
>
> Galatians 5:19-21

Paul is determined to protect oneness, saying that those who consistently and deliberately undermine oneness should be rejected.

> *But avoid foolish controversies and genealogies and strife and disputes about the Law, for they are unprofitable and worthless. Reject a factious man after a first and second warning, knowing that such a man is perverted and is sinning, being self-condemned.*
>
> Titus 3:9-11

As we begin the conversation of being radically restored to oneness with one another, what value do you place on being one with God and, therefore, others? I suggest that ONENESS is one of, if not THE highest value God lives from and through. And yet, after following Jesus for 40 years, it is a value that I see God's people at best ignoring and at worst destroying.

We are made in the image of God, and as such, the absolute truth is that we are made for community. As humans, we often live focused primarily on "I", so the "we" of community needs to be an intentional choice to add something. If we live outside of community, we are simply selling ourselves short. We are made in the image of community.

Jesus modelled living through oneness with God (John 5:19-21). Jesus lived fully aware He was one with God and prayed we would live in oneness with God and one another (John 17:20-24). So, Jesus has sent us into the world *in* oneness and *to live in* oneness (John 17:18). A.J Swoboda puts it this way: 'The triune Godhead is coeternal. God is, in himself, relational. God is ontologically relationship, that is, God does not have relationships; God IS relationship.'[5]

The New Testament commandment, the greater commandment, that we are to 'love one another, as I have loved you' (John 13: 34), clearly indicates that because we are one with God, we are called to be one with one another. Both

---
5 Swoboda, A.J., Subversive Sabbath, Baker Publishing Group, Michigan, 2018, pg 67

Peter and Paul understood this vital key to God's kingdom coming to the world through the people of God.

The centrality and necessity of growing in our knowledge of being one with God is explored in-depth in 2 Peter, helping us to recognize and then practice the qualities that result in us being one with one another. Peter is acutely aware of the importance of living in oneness with God and unity with one another. He is deeply concerned about the influence of false prophets taking his readers away from these things:

> *But false prophets also arose among the people, just as there will also be false teachers among you, who will secretly introduce destructive heresies, even denying the Master who bought them, bringing swift destruction upon themselves.*
>
> 2 Peter 2: 1

Focused on the second coming of Jesus, Peter wants to ensure that his readers are found to be living from their oneness with God and in oneness with one another.

> *But the day of the Lord will come like a thief, in which the heavens will pass away with a roar and the elements will be destroyed with intense heat, and the earth and its works will be burned up.*
>
> *Since all these things are to be destroyed in this way, what sort of people ought you to be in holy conduct and godliness,*
>
> 2 Peter 3: 10 – 11

In this letter, Peter implores them to 'be on guard, so they are not carried away by the error of unprincipled men and fall from your own steadfastness' (2 Pet. 3: 17). Peter is highlighting that they know what they should be looking for and to 'be diligent to be found in Him in peace, spotless and blameless' (1 Pet. 2: 21).

These verses from chapters two and three of 2 Peter come after the discourse of chapter one. As previously noted in the Preface, Peter describes how we have become one with God in verses two to four of chapter one. Then, in verse five, he begins with, 'For this very reason….'. This statement begs the question: *for what reason?* The answer: because we are one with God, we are to pursue oneness with one another. For Peter, this is the outworking of the holy commandment that has been handed on. That is, love one another as I have loved you.

INTRODUCTION

The book of Ephesians is also focused on the deep and vital connection between knowing we have been radically restored to oneness with God and therefore pursuing being radically restored to oneness with one another.

Ephesians 1:1 to 2:10 thoroughly explores the truth, reality, consequences, and outcomes of being restored to oneness with God. Chapter 1, verses 1-14, is rich and pregnant with the extraordinary and monumental changes that occur to our identity in, and status with, God when we are born again:

— we are blessed with every spiritual blessing;

— we are chosen;

— we are holy and blameless before Him;

— we are loved;

— we are adopted into God's family;

— we are redeemed;

— we are forgiven of all our trespasses;

— we can know the mystery of His will;

— we have obtained an inheritance; and

— we are sealed with the Holy Spirit of promise.

Chapter 1, verses 15-23, carry one of Paul's apostolic prayers. A prayer that we would move through life with a spirit of wisdom and revelation in the knowledge of Jesus. Paul longs that we would know and comprehend what has been brought about in Jesus, that we have been forever changed through Him in our salvation. That is, we have been made one with God.

Chapter 2, verses 1-10, describes how we become one with God. That is, 'it is by grace that you have been saved.'

Ephesians 2:11 begins with the word 'therefore'. This signifies that Paul is transitioning from the idea of our oneness with God to ideas around knowing and learning how to live in oneness with one another. Most importantly, Paul is describing the outworking of being one with God. That is, what should naturally follow from our oneness with God is that we live with a commitment to valuing one another. As Jesus said, the way I have loved you — becoming one with you — is how you are to love one another — becoming one with others.

Paul's focus on being one with others begins with the cultural schism between Jews and Gentiles. He highlights that the church is a place where we are fitted together and built together. In chapter three of Ephesians, Paul continues to expand on the idea of oneness with one another with two reasons for the need for oneness.

Paul's first reason is found in his exploration of the significance of his insight into the mystery of Christ. The mystery that in Christ, Gentiles are fellow members of the body and fellow partakers of the promises. This mystery is to be administrated by the church, God's people. This declares to the demonic realm that where they could not live in oneness with God — they rebelled and fell from heaven — the redeemed in Jesus can both live in oneness with God and with one another. The wisdom of God being that loving relationships are the centre and meaning of all life in God's kingdom. Always have been and always will be, as evidenced by Jesus' prayer:

> "I do not ask on behalf of these alone, but for those also who believe in Me through their word; that they may all be one; even as You, Father, **are** in Me and I in You, that they also may be in Us, so that the world may believe that You sent Me."

John 17:20-21

Paul's second reason for the need for, and the importance of, becoming one with one another leads him to pray. He prays that our inner world, the knowledge we hold in our hearts, would be strengthened and transformed by encounters and experiences with Jesus' love. Paul knows that we have moved from the old covenant to the new. We are to love others from the love we have received from Jesus (love one another as I have loved you – John 13:34), no longer loving others from the knowledge we have in loving ourselves (the second of the two great Old Testament commandments – Matthew 22:34-40). The knowledge we have in loving ourselves is corrupted by fear and false self-images we pursue in order to get others to love us. Paul is convinced that God is able, beyond all we could ask or think, to work in our hearts through His power. His purpose is that we can comprehend by experiencing the vast nature of God's love. This was what happened for me in New Zealand.

Paul begins chapter 4 of Ephesians with another 'therefore'. Paul continues to build a case for the importance of discovering how to love one another and live in oneness with one another. It is so critical and vital to the role of God's people on the earth. Consequently, he 'implores' us to walk in a manner worthy of the calling—the calling being: *to live in oneness with God and oneness with one another.* Paul emphasizes how significant our oneness with one another is when he states this requires our diligence. He then defines, with incisive clarity, the places of oneness that are at the core of our shared faith in Jesus.

> *Therefore I, the prisoner of the Lord, implore you to walk in a manner worthy of the calling with which you have been called, with all humility and gentleness, with patience, showing tolerance for one another in love, being diligent to preserve the unity of the Spirit in the bond of peace. There is one body and one Spirit, just as also you were called in one hope of your calling; one Lord, one faith, one baptism, one God and Father of all who is over all and through all and in all.*
>
> Eph. 4: 1 – 6

Paul describes in detail our oneness with God (Eph. 1:1 – 2:10). He then profoundly illustrates the consequential realities and need for oneness with one another (Eph. 2:11 – 4:6). Paul moves to the place of gifted leaders in the body of Christ, being called to equip God's people to live for the service of oneness — 'for the equipping of the saints for the work of service' (Eph. 4: 7 – 16).

Paul then describes how our new life in Christ is to express itself in the practical outworking of living in oneness with others across the board in all of life. In marriage, in family, and if you are a servant. (Eph. 4: 17 – 6: 9).

Finally, in the context of being radically restored to oneness with God and one another, Paul addresses the role of spiritual warfare, requests for prayer and closing relational thoughts (Eph. 6: 10 – 24).

LIFE TOGETHER IN THE NEW TESTAMENT

Upon returning from New Zealand, I began to see the strength of the connection between experiencing the love of God and oneness with Him and living in oneness with one another. The New Testament writers clearly understood the significance of the New Testament commandment. Previously, I had been aware that there are over fifty references in the New Testament about how we are to live with one another. However, this new perspective and level of awareness brought me to see these references in light of an overarching narrative for New Testament living; that the knowledge of our restored oneness with God leads to our pursuit of oneness with one another. This fits with an overarching narrative of the whole bible that acknowledges the need for forgiveness of sin in the context of breaking relationship with God and others.

However, for many Christians, the overarching biblical narrative is that God has legislated, rather than described, what behavior is required to remain in right relationship with Him. When sin is viewed as rebellion against God, it can lead to a legal or forensic approach to sin. The emphasis here can characterize God using rules and regulations to restrain bad behavior and exercise power over people. Invariably, it focuses on people's behavior and activity and God's assessment of its appropriateness.

The creation story begins with God as a community of covenant love who desires to expand the circle of this family with a core expression of covenant love. Here sin is not a legal matter as much as it is a relational one. Sin is not falling short of rules and regulations but rather a falling short of expressing love. Consequently, our walk with God fits a relational expression and nature more than a judicial one.[6]

This is why Paul does not appeal to an ethical system in how we live with others.

George Ladd[7] helps us here when he writes:

> This can easily be illustrated by the most casual reading of Paul's lists of virtues. The "fruit of the Spirit" in Galatians 5:22, 23 is often taken as normative for Paul's concept of the good Christian life, but these virtues must be compared with the similar lists in Philippians 4:8 and Colossians 3: 12-15. There is no overlapping between the list in Philippians and the other two lists, and there are only four virtues that occur more than once: love, kindness, meekness, and longsuffering. Such lists do not offer a formal ethic, nor are they designed to portray the pattern of the good person or the Christian ideal toward which all are to strive. They are rather different ways Paul addresses himself to concrete historical situations to explain how the new life in Christ is to express itself.

So, when it comes to our life with one another, Paul considers how our new life in Christ should manifest itself.

The 'one another's' of the New Testament are not to be seen as one of a plethora of activities to tick off in the Christian life. They are to be the primary outworking of our spirituality. Galatians 3:26 – 29 makes this link abundantly clear:

---

6   Righteousness and justification do have an element of legal and judicial meaning in both their Hebrew and Greek terms. However, as I will explore shortly, in the Old Testament, righteousness emphasises relationship with God in the context of covenant.
7   Ladd. G.E., (1993). A Theology of the New Testament, Wm. B. Eerdmans Publishing Co, pg 556

INTRODUCTION

> *For you are all sons of God through faith in Christ Jesus. For all of you who were baptized into Christ have clothed yourselves with Christ. There is neither Jew nor Greek, there is neither slave nor free man, there is neither male nor female; for you are all one in Christ Jesus. And if you belong to Christ, then you are Abraham's descendants, heirs according to promise.*

We belong to Jesus collectively; therefore, we are members of one another (Eph. 4: 25). The strength and significance of these truths is brought into clear and resounding focus by Jesus himself when He declares:

> *"By this all men will know that you are My disciples, if you have love for one another."*

John 13: 35

and when He prays:

> *"I do not ask on behalf of these alone, but for those also who believe in Me through their word; that they may all be one; even as You, Father, are in Me and I in You, that they also may be in Us, so that the world may believe that You sent Me."*

John 17: 20 – 21.

However, for many of God's people, this truth of being members of one another has a limited expression in daily life. This can be for many different reasons, including the adherence to an overarching bible narrative focusing on personal outcomes over community life and the influence of individualism as the primary frame of reference in relationships.

Being a disciple of Jesus in western culture demands the need to revisit the influence of individualism. The cultural power of individualism can diminish and even eradicate the truth that we are members of one another and that we belong to Jesus. That we have been restored to God's covenant community of love.

A follower of Jesus must resist the cultural influence of individualism and resist the works of darkness that are motivated by 'self'. Satan conceived and created the motivation toward self-gratification and individualism. He led a rebellion of angels based on self-will, self-exultation, self-enthronement, and self-deification.

> *But you said in your heart,*
> *'I will ascend to heaven;*
> *I will raise my throne above the stars of God,*
> *And I will sit on the mount of assembly*
> *In the recesses of the north.*
> *I will ascend above the heights of the clouds;*
> *I will make myself like the Most High.'*

Isaiah 14:13 – 14.

The demonic realm tempts mankind to follow them through becoming self-reliant and self-centered, believing they can be like God and make their own judgements.[8] They create a desire in people to make God in the image they choose.

As followers of Jesus, we have been restored to the family of God, empowered by the Holy Spirit and given grace to live through covenant love in communion with God and others. We belong to Jesus and are members of one another. It is our great privilege to love one another as Jesus loves us because we are under the law of Christ.

THE LAW OF CHRIST

Paul describes himself as being under the law of Christ (1 Cor. 9:21) and fulfilling the law of Christ (Gal. 6:2). This is the law of love as set out in the New Testament commandment. Paul has come to see that because Jesus has brought the Law as a way to attain righteousness to its end, that God has now chosen perfect love over perfect ethics. God is a God of love whose love covers a multitude of sins as He patiently leads us towards His ideal of who we can be.

Gregory Boyd[9] describes it this way:

> God not only accommodates us in our fallen condition, *he becomes one of us* in the midst of our fallen condition. God not only accommodates us in the midst of our sin, *he becomes our sin* (2 Cor: 5:21). God not only works with us in our banishment from Paradise, *he becomes our banishment from Paradise*. God not only works with us in our separation, *he becomes our separation from God*. He not only continues to love us within the curse under which we live, *he becomes our curse*.

---

8 Genesis 3:5 notes the temptation to be like God knowing good from evil. Satan wanted Adam and Eve to exchange their oneness with God for being like God.
9 Boyd. G., (2004) Repentance of Religion. Baker Books, pg 176-177

INTRODUCTION

Nothing could be further from God's ideal than to become *the opposite* of his ideal—to become sin, banishment, separation, the curse. Yet this is precisely what the Lord does for us and in doing this, God clothes us with His righteousness in the midst of our shame. God covers a great multitude of sins—in principle, all sin—with his love.

Sin is when we fall short of God's created purpose for us. It is a failure to reflect the dignity and splendour of God's image as we were created to do. The glory we are to reflect is the love of God, and since reflecting love involves relationship, falling short of God's glory means falling short of the kind of *agape* love relationship that we are created for. Reflecting God's image or glo-ry requires us, as mirrors, to be in a particular relationship with the object we are reflecting. Sin carries the idea of broken relationship with God Himself rather than merely breaking the rules of God. If this is the case, the problem is actually the glory humanity has lost due to a broken relationship with God rather than the punishment we receive from guilt due to broken rules. As such, righteousness in a relational paradigm, being set right or the setting right of relationship, makes more sense as a solution: forgiveness, reconciliation, and reunion with God.[10]

God's righteousness is not primarily an ethical quality but rather the characteristics or action of how God deals rightly within that relationship.[11]

As we consider how we allow our new life in Christ to express itself, it is necessary to acknowledge a tension the writers of the New Testament faced in adequately describing the dynamic we all face. That dynamic is the tension between the indicative and the imperative. The indicative involves the affirmation of what God has done in us. The imperative involves the exhortation to live out this new life in our circumstances and relationships. As such, there are a range of motivations in the New Testament for our human response to what God has done as we manifest our new life in relationships with others.

The primary motivation, as has already been established, is love. However, our life with one another is also enabled by the life of the Spirit that indwells us (Rom. 8:3-4; Gal.5:14). This life is evidenced by the presence of the fruit of the Spirit (Gal. 5:20). Equally, while Paul does not hold up the earthly life of Jesus as a standard of moral excellence, he does call us to imitate Jesus' love in giving ourselves for the benefit of others (Phil. 2:1-11).

---

10 Callaghan. J.M., (2020). *Covenantal Faithfulness and Relational Righteousness*, Masters Thesis Luther Theological Seminary, pg 29
11 *Dictionary of Paul and His Letters: a compendium of Contemporary Biblical Scholarship*, Edited by: Hawthorne, G.F., Martin, R.P., and Reid, D.G., Intervarsity Press, pg 829

We are to walk in the newness of life as we have identified with His death and resurrection through baptism (Rom.6: 3-4). We have been raised up into this new life, and where we were once dead in our sins, we are now alive with Christ, living for the work He has prepared beforehand (Eph. 2: 1 -10). Finally, in a similar way, because we have been made holy and blameless (Eph. 1: 4, Col. 1: 22), we are sanctified, having been set apart to be God's people. At the same time, scripture calls for a human response to yield to the ways of God and embrace holiness (Rom. 6: 19; 1 Thess. 4:7). Not as a way of designating growth in ethical conduct but rather as a way of expressing our new life in Christ.

We are not to live with one another through adherence to ethical standards. Instead, we are to live by following the Spirit, loving people where they are in all its complexity. Ethical truth is not to be based on circumstances, but it is to be subservient to love. Indeed, this is the way Jesus loved prostitutes, tax collectors, and the broken. Think here of the woman caught in adultery or the woman at the well. We have been called to radical restoration with others that can only be accomplished if we view ourselves and others through the lens of how Jesus loved us — 'while we were yet sinners, Christ died for us.' (Rom. 5:8)

SUMMARY

— If we live outside of community, we are selling ourselves short, for we are made in the image of community.

— We have been made to be one with God, and we are called to be one with one another.

— Sin is to be viewed as a relational matter before but not without being a legal matter. Sin is not falling short of the rules and regulations but rather a falling short of expressing love.

— The cultural power of individualism can diminish and eradicate the truth that we are members of one another.

— God's righteousness is not primarily an ethical quality but rather the character or action of how God deals rightly with any relationship.

— Ethical truth is not to be based on circumstances, but it is to be subservient to love.

INTRODUCTION

QUESTIONS AND ACTIVITIES

1. How have you benefited from being in community?

2. How have you been disappointed or hurt through engaging in community? How have you overcome or walked through that hurt?

3. Can you identify two ways in which you fall short in expressing love that you want to change and that you would ask Jesus to help you grow and improve in?

4. Can you name two belief systems you hold from the cultural influence towards individualism that undermine your pursuit of being in community?

Chapter 1

THE CALL TO LOVE OTHERS

...practicing our spirituality in community

— Loving others is a Kingdom principle and commandment that our brains have actually been wired for in creation.

— Understanding the truth that righteousness is both right standing with God and living in right relationship enables us to embrace the New Testament commandment.

— Adopting the mindset of a strong group culture will enhance our understanding of the New Testament 'one anothers.'

— Establishing and living in community that empowers spiritual formation for all.

US TWO
by A.A. Milne

Wherever I am, there's always Pooh,
There's always Pooh and Me.
Whatever I do, he wants to do,
"Where are you going today?" says Pooh:
"Well, that's very odd 'cos I was too.
Let's go together," says Pooh, says he.
"Let's go together," says Pooh.

"What's twice eleven?" I said to Pooh.
("Twice what?" said Pooh to Me.)
"I think it ought to be twenty-two."
"Just what I think myself," said Pooh.
"It wasn't an easy sum to do,
But that's what it is," said Pooh, said he.
"That's what it is," said Pooh.

"Let's look for dragons," I said to Pooh.
"Yes, let's," said Pooh to Me.
We crossed the river and found a few –
"Yes, those are dragons all right," said Pooh.
"As soon as I saw the beasts I knew.
That's what they are," said Pooh.

"Let's frighten the dragons," I said to Pooh.
"That's right," said Pooh to Me.
"I'm not afraid," I said to Pooh,
And I held his paw and shouted "Shoo!
Silly old dragons!" – and off they flew.

"I wasn't afraid," said Pooh, said he,
"I'm never afraid with you."
So wherever I am, there's always Pooh,
There's always Pooh and Me.
"What would I do?" I said to Pooh,
"If it wasn't for you," and Pooh said: "True,
It isn't much fun for One, but Two,
Can stick together, says Pooh, says he. "That's how it is,"
Can stick together, says Pooh, says he. "That's how it is," says Pooh[1]

---

[1] Milne. A. A., (1927). First published in Now We Are Six, Methuen & Co.

CHAPTER 1

PURSUING LOVING RELATIONSHIPS

This delightful conversation between Christopher Robin and Pooh Bear expresses an innocence we long for in relationships. However, real-life is more complicated than this. Our relationships suffer from varying degrees of tension, anger, disappointment, and frustration. Relationships can be chaotic and can bring chaos into our life experiences.

Psalm 34:14 in the Passion Translation[2] encourages us to:

> *Keep turning your back on every sin,*
> *and make "peace" your life motto.*
> *Practice being at peace with everyone.*

The footnotes in The Passion Translation provide the following reflection on the use of the word 'peace' in this verse:

> Twice the Hebrew uses the word *shalom*. This word means much more than peace. It means wholeness, wellness, well-being, safe, happy, friendly, favor, completeness, to make peace, peace offering, secure, to prosper, to be victorious, to be content, tranquil, quiet, and restful. The pictographic symbols for the word shalom (*shin, lamed, vav, mem*) read "Destroy the authority that binds to chaos." The noun *shalom* is derived from the verbal root *shalom*, which means "to restore," in the sense of replacing or providing what is needed in order to make someone or something whole and complete. So, *shalom* is used to describe those of us who have been provided all that is needed to be whole and complete and break off all authority that would attempt to bind us to chaos.

The beatitudes in Matthew 5:3-11 offer a description of how God's Kingdom works. They are a manifesto for Kingdom living. They present a whole new way of being human.

Matthew 5:9 calls followers of Jesus to take the posture of being peacemakers.

> *Blessed are the peacemakers, for they shall be called sons of God.*

The consequence of being a peacemaker is that we bear the image of God, 'for they shall be called sons of God.' Our goal & purpose is to grow in Christ to be more complete image-bearers.

---

[2] Simmons. B., translator. The Passion Translation®, (2017). BroadStreet Publishing® Group, LLC.

> *For those whom He foreknew, He also predestined to become conformed to the image of His Son, so that He would be the firstborn among many brethren;*
>
> Romans 8:29

Peacemakers actively seek reconciliation (Colossians 1:20). They take the initiative to love well in the chaos of conflict, tension, and disagreement. Peacemakers move towards chaos to create peace and build bridges. On the other hand, peacekeepers avoid the chaos and conflict. They can neglect pursuing the hard work of finding wholeness that marks a life of flourishing and shalom, instead pursuing compromises leaving tension points unresolved.

Seeking to grow in the practice of loving others is a Kingdom principle seen throughout the Word of God. To fulfil this practice, we need to start with pursuing being whole and complete ourselves so that we do not contribute to chaos in relationships. We commit ourselves to the pursuit of shalom, which includes restoring things to the way they were originally intended to be.[3]

THE PLACE OF NEUROSCIENCE

Restoring everything to the way God originally intended it to be for us individually presupposes the need for spiritual formation. Spiritual formation is the lifelong pursuit of becoming more like Jesus in our daily lives. It begins and is sustained by loving devotion and attachment to Jesus.

> *"If you love Me, you will keep My commandments."*
>
> John 14:15
>
> *"He who has My commandments and keeps them is the one who loves Me; and he who loves Me will be loved by My Father, and I will love him and will disclose Myself to him."*
>
> John 14:21

However, in my 35 years of experience as a pastor, I have found the practices of loving others like Jesus and empowering others in their spiritual formation confusing. Some people progress well year in and year out in their spiritual formation. Others get stuck, resigning themselves to being disappointed and discouraged. Still, others get stuck and, in their frustration, slowly lose their

---

3 Shalom is a manifestation of 'echad'. Shalom is the result of echads work.

devotion to Jesus. For so many years, this confused me. What happened differently in each of these situations?

Scientific research in neuropsychology and brain development provides helpful insights into understanding what is occurring in the process of spiritual formation. Jim Wilder and Michel Hendricks[4] provided a significant 'light bulb' moment for me as I read the following:

> Most phones have two processors running simultaneously. One handles the cell phone communication. The second processor runs everything else. The human brain also has two processors, one on the right and another on the left, that work together but specialize in different responsibilities.
>
> There is a popular misconception in our culture about the left and right sides of the brain. I understood that the right side was creative and the left was analytical, and some people were left-brain dominant while others were right-brain dominant. Artists and musicians were right brained, and accountants and engineers were left-brained. That was not an accurate description.
>
> All of the ways in which we interpret our world, from seeing an expression on a friend's face to smelling our grandmother's roast chicken cooking in the oven, enter into our dual processor brain on the back of the right side. Processing the smell of the chicken shifts from the back to the front of the right side, and somewhere behind our right eye it crosses over to the left side. Then the smell of grandma's chicken processes from the front to the back on the left side. It's like going up one supermarket aisle and then crossing over and returning on the next aisle to the left. Everything takes a path. Words in a conversation. A handshake. A favourite song. A puzzled look on a friend's face. A math problem. The taste of grandma's chicken when you finally sit down and eat. That and everything else you experience follows this path. Back to front on the right side, front to back on the left side
>
> The right side starts processing our surroundings and draws conclusions before the left side is even aware of what is happening. Jim calls this "pre-conscious thought", meaning that our right brain

---

4   Hendricks. M., & Wilder. J., (2020). *The Other Half of Church: Christian Community, brain science and overcoming spiritual stagnation.* Moody Publishers, Chicago, pg 19-26

processes our surroundings faster and before our conscious awareness. The right hemisphere process that creates our working identity integrates our reality six times per second. The brain brings together current experience and emotionally important personal memories to create an active sense of who we are in our relationships at that moment. This happens faster than we can become conscious, so we assume we just 'know' who we are at all times.

The right brain functions begin with our important relational attachments and are intended to help us be ourselves in relationships. The right side, the "fast track" and the left side the "slow track". The right hemisphere is a more powerful processor than the left and samples our environment at six times a second. The left side samples at five times a second, so we often know things faster than we are conscious of them and definitely faster than we can speak about them. We might say the right brain has more horsepower. From a theological point of view, God put a lot of power into the responsibilities dominant in the right side of our brains. These functions must be important to Him and crucial to our ability to grow as disciples of Jesus.

With that in mind, our right brain governs the whole range of relational life: who we love, our emotional reactions to our surroundings, our ability to calm ourselves, and our identity, both as individuals and as a community. The right side manages our strongest relational connections, (both to people and God) and our experience of emotional connectedness to others. *And character formation.* If we want to grow and transform our character into the character of Jesus, we must involve activities that stimulate and develop the right brain.

The left side of the brain is what we commonly think of as "the mind" in popular culture. Our concept of the mind describes only half of our brain. The left brain is dominant for functions we associate with the mind: logical thinking, problem solving, strategies, and language. Cause-and-effect relationships are formed here. Words are put to our life experiences to create autobiographical stories. Problems are solved. Plans are hatched. Arguments are formulated. Stories are told. Truth is defended. What we think of as "the mind" covers only one half of the brain—the left brain. The left brain runs at the speed of words; the right brain runs at the speed of joy.

CHAPTER 1

God designed our left brain to understand important aspects of our Christian beliefs. Without truth we would be lost. Our beliefs and doctrine (formulated in the left brain) are created from knowing the relational love of God (formulated in the right brain). The right brain is the fast track, and it leads the left brain. This means that a smoothly running right hemisphere is necessary for our entire brain to function as designed.

Left-brained discipleship emphasizes beliefs, doctrine, willpower, and strategies but neglects right-brain loving attachments, joy, emotional development, and identity. Ignoring right-brained relational development creates Christians who believe in God's love but have difficulty experiencing it in daily life, especially during distress.

I am not suggesting that the familiar left-brain strategies are unimportant in discipleship. Biblical teaching, Scripture meditations, beliefs, strategies, and the choices we make play an essential role in forming our character. We don't grow without developing these left-brain skills.

However, without the proper right-brained relational and emotional environment, our fruit will be meagre. When the right brain and the left brain work together in harmony, character transformation becomes commonplace in our communities.

Scientific research in neuropsychology and brain development is also enlightening in understanding how our pursuit of loving relationships is undermined by our emotional trigger points.[5]

God has created the brain, that among other things, houses a 'parent' and a 'child' part of the brain.

The limbic system, our subconscious, gathers and processes information. It creates software programs for memories, habits, emotions, pleasure, things that excite you, your drives, desires, pain and survival strategies.

---

[5] The following ideas are drawn from the notes used by Dr. Dianne Grocott in a seminar presentation in May 2017, Melbourne, Australia.

"PARENT" AND "CHILD" PARTS OF THE BRAIN

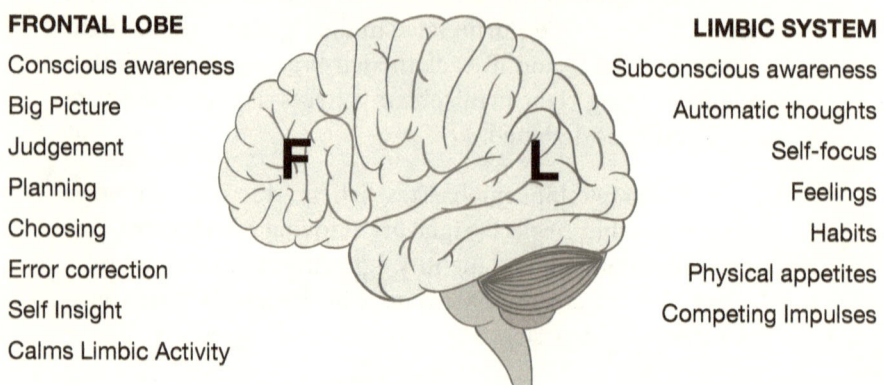

FRONTAL LOBE
Conscious awareness
Big Picture
Judgement
Planning
Choosing
Error correction
Self Insight
Calms Limbic Activity

LIMBIC SYSTEM
Subconscious awareness
Automatic thoughts
Self-focus
Feelings
Habits
Physical appetites
Competing Impulses

The limbic system is made up of:

— Thalamus: all information goes through the thalamus and it decides what information is sent to consciousness (inner room switchboard).

— Amygdala: watches all memories and determines if I am safe and need to call on coping mechanisms to be secure (the guardian).

— Locus Ceruleus: monitors what help is needed and informs our reactions of fright, flight or fight through being alert, watchful and careful (panic button).

— Hippocampus: registers new information (especially emotionally charged), send information to long term storage and retrieves memories (memory maker).

— Nucleus Accumbens: the source of dopamine release attached to good feelings creating an impulse to repeat the behaviour (pleasure centre).

The frontal lobe calms and directs the limbic system. It is still under development until our mid-twenties, sees the big picture with problems and solutions, sees good and bad making choices between them, and is essential for relationships. It is the place of learning where our values and choices are formed and informed. It can be rewired by biological, psychological and spiritual factors throughout life through self-awareness and personal responsibility (mindfulness) and our choices to change.

The frontal lobe has four centres:

— The thinker: where reasoning, planning, thinking and strategizing take place and needs to be fed with the truth, wisdom and insight.

— Other Centredness: where our capacity for love, empathy and compassion reside, seeing the perspective of others and choosing right from wrong.

— Conscience: the place of ethical decision making and conviction of guilt.

— Brakes: recognises and inhibits inappropriate behaviour.

From these insights we understand our spiritual formation in pursuing loving relationships and being one with others recognises two things.

First, when the Limbic system rules our life, our behaviour and habits are being formed by impulses, not out of conscious thoughtful decision making. Our subconscious emerges in our conscious world in eruptions of fear, anxiety, pleasure, memories, wants, feeling of self-consciousness, important, unimportance, shame and panic. The 'child' part of our brain overtakes us.

> *"When I was a child I spoke like a child, I thought like a child, I reasoned like a child. When I became a man, I gave up childish ways."*
>
> 1 Corinthians 13:11

Second, for the Frontal lobe to parent the child in the ways of God's Kingdom resulting in loving relationships and oneness, Jesus must be the guide in its development and rewiring. The gospel must be the school master with biblical love being the plumbline and the fruit of the Spirit the outcome.

Scientific research in neuropsychology and brain development is also enlightening when considering the pursuit of shalom. Researchers are discovering that the human brain is soft wired for sociability, attachment, affection, and companionship. God originally intended for people to respond to one another with empathy.

These ideas come from the discovery of mirror neurons. Through MRI technology, researchers can show that when we observe another's emotional response, we can have the same experience. For example, when we observe someone else's frustration, anger, or joy, the same neurons that are lighting up in their brains, also light up in ours. We experience another's reality as if it were our own.

The research suggests that we are not naturally predisposed to anger, violence, or self-interest. These feelings and their associated actions are learned and become wired into our brains through observation. The chaos these behaviours bring to relationships does not reflect God's creative intent. God, in creating people, soft-wired our brains for sociability, attachment, affection, and companionship. Our natural drive is to belong in loving relationships.

THE PLACE OF RIGHTEOUSNESS

Understanding the deeply embedded Jewish cultural concept of righteousness from the Old Testament will help us immensely to live out the practice of loving others. The writing of Achtemeier[6] helps us understand this concept:

> "Righteousness", as it is understood in the Old Testament, is a thoroughly Hebraic concept, foreign to the Western mind and at variance with the common understanding of the term. The failure to comprehend its meaning is perhaps most responsible for the view of the Old Testament religion as 'legalistic' and as far removed from the graciousness of the New Testament.
>
> Rather, "righteousness" is, in the Old Testament, the fulfilment of the demands of a relationship, whether that relationship be with men or with God. Each man is set within a multitude of relationships: king with people, judge with family, tribesman with community, community with resident alien and poor all with God. And each of these relationships brings with it specific demands, the fulfilment of which constitutes righteousness.

For the ancient Hebrews, righteousness was a relational term. God's righteousness is His relentless willingness to forgive, reconcile and set right our relationship with Him. The Old Testament reveals a firm commitment from God to relational reconciliation.[7] As Boyd reminds us:

---

6   Achtemeier. E.R., ed. Buttrich. G.A., (1962). *The Interpreter's Dictionary of the Bible – Volume 4*; Abingdon Press, pg 80-85

7   The classic reformed perspective insists that justification is a "declarative, judicial verdict, not a process," and thus cannot be "anything else other than the courtroom declaration that someone is righteous before God." See Michael S. Horton, "traditional Reformed View," in *Justification: Five Views* edited by James K. Beilby and Paul Rhodes Eddy, (Downers Grove, IL: InterVarsity Press, 2011), 93. To be clear, this argument is not predicated upon a claim that there is not any element of legal or judicial meaning in both the Hebrew and Greek uses of righteousness/justice/justification. However, it is undeniable the in the OT, righteousness, "emphasizes the relational aspect of God and humanity in the context of a covenant." See M.T. Brauch and K.L. Onesti, "Righteousness, Righteousness of God," in *Dictionary of Paul and His Letters: A Compendium of Contemporary Biblical Scholarship*, edited by Gerald F. Hawthorn, Ralph P. Martin and Daniel G. Reid (Downers Grove, IL: InterVarsity Press, 1993, 828. (These ideas came from Tim Callaghan, *Covenantal Faithfulness and Relational Righteousness*, Master Thesis, Luther Theological Seminary, May 2020, pg 868)

> People who read Scripture sympathetically generally find that the God of the Old Testament is by-and-large a relational God of hesed (i.e., covenant-love) who continually strives to bring all people... into relationships of shalom and covenantal righteousness/justice with himself as well as with each other.[8]

When Paul uses the word righteousness, He means right relationship with God. Barclay makes the point that:

> We must not confuse or conflate "right relationship" with God as "right standing" which brings unfortunate forensic undertones to an idea that is not about our guilty status as sinners, but the removal of sin so that relationship might be restored between God and humanity. This better aligns with the consistent NT theme of freedom from bondage to sin and the Enemy. Sin is a barrier to relationship, but not because God cannot look upon sin, but rather because sin separates us from God's ideal design and purpose for relationship with God. More importantly, sin is the human rejection of God's desire for relationship. Sin is when humans fail to live out our end of covenant relationship with God. Thus, God takes on human flesh, to fulfill the human obligations for a faithful relationship with their God. The idea of guilt, which is present in the New Testament witness, is about wronging another as well as about your human susceptibility to feel shame for our sin (See Hebrews 10:22 for the idea of sin and our guilty consciences). This shame is often used by Satan and/or others to accuse and condemn us.[9]

Fred Faller[10] explores this concept in relationship to Jesus when he writes:

> Jesus lived out this kind of righteousness with a passion that confounded many of the people around him. While the Pharisees were muttering about the character of the woman who was washing Jesus' feet with perfume, Jesus was caring about her, thus meeting the simple demands of the relationship. When Zaccheus climbed the tree just to get a glimpse of Jesus, Jesus met that anticipation by having lunch with the man and his family while the Jews stood outside and pondered Jesus' poor choice of friends. He initiated with the woman

---

8 Boyd, G.A., (2017). *Crucifixion of the Warrior God: Interpreting the Old Testament's Violent Portraits of God in Light of the Cross. Vol 1: The Cruciform Hermeneutic*, Fortress Press, pg 281
9 Barclay. W., *The Letter to the Romans (Revised Edition): The Daily Study Bible Series*, 5.
10 Faller. F., (2017). Disciples Today, *Right or Righteousness* retrieved from www.disciplestoday.org/bible-study/digging-deeper/item-8714-right-or-righteous on September 6th 2021

at the well, while the disciples could not figure out why he would be talking to a woman. Jesus stopped amid the throng to meet the needs of a bleeding woman when she cried out for attention by simply touching his garments. Jesus saw that right relationships were the key to righteousness, rather than legalistically and dutifully acting out some prescribed behavior.

That which builds up and promotes unity is righteous. Whatever breaks down or degrades a relationship is unrighteous. This does not mean that tough conversations are to be avoided. Instead, we approach a tough conversation with the goal of ensuring the other person knows and is convinced that we love them, not that they're convinced we're right. It is possible to be 'right' and, simultaneously, unrighteous.

Matthew 10:37–38 teaches us that the demands of one relationship can come into conflict with the demands of another.

> "He who loves father or mother more than Me is not worthy of Me; and he who loves son or daughter more than Me is not worthy of Me. And he who does not take his cross and follow after Me is not worthy of Me."

However, the righteous choice is always the one that places our relationship with God first.

In our relationships with others, it is imperative to remember that our righteousness in God is only because we are forgiven (Eph.2:8–9). Therefore, our righteousness with others must be focused on sustaining the relationship through grace and forgiveness, not exercising our sense of justice. Dunn puts it this way: 'God is just not because he acts in accordance with some outdated ideal of justice, but because He has acted in fulfilment of the obligation he took upon Himself as covenant God of Israel.'[11]

Isaiah 9:7 tells us that Jesus will establish and uphold His Kingdom with justice and righteousness.

> *There will be no end to the increase of His government or of peace,*
> *On the throne of David and over his kingdom,*
> *To establish it and to uphold it with justice and righteousness*
> *From then on and forevermore.*
> *The zeal of the Lord of hosts will accomplish this.*

---

11 Dunn. James D.G., *World Biblical Commentary*, Authentic Media, 38a: Romans 1-8, pg 174

A complete understanding of this fact will ensure that we play our part in the development and significance of the church as a community.

JESUS AND THE CALL TO LOVING COMMUNITIES

God is a family (The Trinity) who makes family. God is love, and love cannot exist without relationship. In Mark 3:31-35, we find clues to how Jesus saw the call to practising love for one another in community.

> *Then His mother and His brothers arrived, and standing outside they sent word to Him and called Him. A crowd was sitting around Him, and they said to Him, "Behold, Your mother and Your brothers are outside looking for You." Answering them, He said, "Who are My mother and My brothers?" Looking about at those who were sitting around Him, He said, "Behold My mother and My brothers! For whoever does the will of God, he is My brother and sister and mother."*

Those listening to Jesus would have been horrified and offended by these comments! Why?

The Jewish culture Jesus was raised in and lived with can be described as a 'strong group culture.' A strong group culture is a commitment to life where a person perceives themselves as a member of the group and is responsible to the group for their actions, destiny, career, and life in general. They were embedded in the group and free to do what was right and necessary only if their decisions were in accord with the group norms and best interests. The needs of the group had priority over the individual member.

As the eldest son of a widow, Jesus was expected to put His family first. As a rabbi, he was undermining the very essence of the Jewish roots for a strong group culture, that is, the family. Jesus was elevating those who did the will of His Father as the group He was embedded in and accountable to. Jesus was, and is, calling His disciples to give up their usual allegiance to blood families to join a multi-ethnic family. If you don't, you cannot be His disciple.

Jesus does not at any stage question a strong group culture approach for His understanding of community. He simply redefines the qualification for being in His strong group style family.

Today, many of us raised in western cultures find it extremely difficult to imagine living in a strong group culture style of community. We have been raised in a 'weak group culture' where the individual has priority over the group. Western culture fights for and demands individualism and tolerates everyone being a critic. We hear the notion of strong group culture through its poorest possible application. At best, that is controlling and, at worst, cultish.

The clash of Kingdom culture and western culture significantly undermines our capacity for, and commitment to community as Jesus sees it. The essence of loving one another, being one with God and one with one another, can be held captive by God's people to the justifications of individualism.

THE ONE ANOTHERS OF THE NEW TESTAMENT

Righteousness is a relational matter before it is an ethical matter. The New Testament writers grasped the deeper Hebrew understanding that righteousness was about living in right relationship before, but not without, right standing. They also imbued their writing with the strong group culture of the Jews that Jesus upheld in His understanding of community. As a result, the New Testament writers set out to describe the values and activities of community life through the use of the phrase 'one another'.

The phrase "one another" is derived from the Greek word *allelon,* which means: "one another; each other; mutually, reciprocally." It occurs 100 times in the New Testament. Approximately 59 of those occurrences are specific commands teaching us how (and how not) to relate to one another. Obedience to those commands is imperative. It forms the basis for all true Christian community and directly impacts our witness to the world (John 13:35). In addition to *allelon*, the Bible uses other words and phrases to instruct us on how to relate to others. The following list of these commands is not exhaustive and primarily focuses on the use of *allelon:*

Positive Commands

Love one another (John 13: 34 – *This command occurs at least 16 times*)
Be devoted to one another (Rom. 12:10)
Honor one another **above yourselves** (Rom. 12:10)
Live in harmony with one another (Rom. 12:16)
Build up one another (Rom. 14:19; 1 Thess. 5:11)
Be like-minded towards one another (Rom. 15:5)
Accept one another (Rom. 15:7)
Admonish one another (Rom. 15:14; Col. 3:16)
Greet one another (Rom. 16:16)
Care for one another (1 Cor.12: 25)
Serve one another (Gal. 5:13)
Bear one another's **burdens** (Gal. 6:2)

Forgive one another (Eph. 4:2, 32; Col. 3:13)
Be patient with one another (Eph. 4:2; Col. 3:13)
Speak the truth in love (Eph. 4:15, 25)
Be kind and compassionate to one another (Eph. 4:32)
Speak to one another **with psalms, hymns, and spiritual songs** (Eph. 5:19)
Submit to one another (Eph. 5:21; 1 Pet. 5:5)
Consider others **better than yourselves** (Phil. 2:3)
Look to the interests of one another (Phil. 2:4)
Bear with one another (Col. 3:13)
Teach one another (Col. 3:16)
Comfort one another (1 Thess. 4:18)
Encourage one another (1 Thess. 5:11)
Exhort one another (Heb. 3:13)
Stir up [provoke, stimulate] one another **to love and good works** (Heb. 10:24)
Show hospitality to one another (1 Pet. 4:9)
Employ the gifts that God has given us for the benefit of one another (1 Pet. 4:10)
Clothe yourselves with humility towards one another (1 Peter 4:10)
Pray for one another (James 5:16)
Confess your faults to one another (James 5:16)

Negative Commands (how *not* to treat one another)

Do not lie to one another (Col. 3: 9)
Stop passing judgment on one another (Rom. 14:13)
If you keep on biting and devouring each other… **you'll be destroyed** by each other (Gal. 5: 15)
Let us **not become conceited, provoking, and envying** each other (Gal. 5:26)
Do not slander one another (James 4:11)
Don't grumble against each other (James 5:9)12

The danger we face as 21st century Christians living in western culture is that we see this list as a set of dos and don'ts. A list of expectations through which we are judged and accused. A list we read through with the lens of needing to stay in right standing to be righteous. However, the writers were Jews who understood righteousness as being more about being in right relationship.

---

12 MMLearn, (n.d). *The One Another Passages*, Retrieved from https://www.mmlearn.org/hubfs/docs/OneAnotherPassages.pdf on September 6th 2021

Equally, they lived with a commitment to a strong group culture focused on serving the group's needs. These two ideas underpin the concept that we are members of one another (Rom.12:5; Eph.4:15). For New Testament believers, 'one another' living was the natural consequence of following Jesus through being led by the Spirit (Rom.8:12-17). They were 'walking out' their faith in their relationship with Jesus. They were not 'working out' their faith through self-effort from a need to perform.

THE HEARTBEAT AND INSTRUCTION FOR 'ONE ANOTHER' LIVING

As we read the values and practices of *allelon* and the call for us to live this way in the writing of the New Testament, there is an evident recurring theme that undergirds it all. It is to make loving one another the focus of our spirituality. The New Testament writings around this idea are rich with insights. Let's explore six of them.

The first insight comes from Paul when he states that loving others is at the centre of his teaching and instruction.

> *But the goal of our instruction is love from a pure heart and a good conscience and a sincere faith.*

> 1 Tim. 1:5

The word 'instruction' can also be translated as 'command'. There is a strength in the centrality that Paul is announcing about love. This strength is accompanied by the qualities that characterise the love Paul requires. That love comes from a pure heart, based in a good conscience and released through a sincere faith. Love that is personal in strength, considered in thoughtfulness, and expressed for empowerment. This love transcends an emotional response based on feelings. It is a love that is based in Kingdom values and application.

The second insight is that we don't love because the Bible tells us to love. We love because of the way God has loved Jesus.

> *Therefore be imitators of God, as beloved children; and walk in love, just as Christ also loved you and gave Himself up for us, an offering and a sacrifice to God as a fragrant aroma.*

> Eph. 5:1-2

CHAPTER 1

We are to do unto others as God has done for us through Jesus. The basis for our behaviour is the sacrificial love of Jesus. We are to pattern the way we treat one another on how we have been treated by God, as His children, included in the family of God.

> *Let all bitterness and wrath and anger and clamor and slander be put away from you, along with all malice. Be kind to one another, tender-hearted, forgiving each other, just as God in Christ also has forgiven you.*
>
> Eph. 4:31-32

The third insight into practicing love for one another is found in Galatians 5:6.

> *For in Christ Jesus neither circumcision nor uncircumcision means anything, but faith working through love.*

Here Paul is diminishing the concept of God conferring status based on approval or disapproval. Instead, he is elevating the relational restoration of the covenant between God and mankind. Faith working through love represents the centrality of active, mature love. This reflects God's nature in all of creation.

When faith is disconnected from love, it can result in an obligation based in human effort. A faith that is described in some circles as: 'name it and claim it'. A faith that is self-oriented and self-serving. This expression of faith creates a focus on living for God's purposes (a vertical morality) that to readily ignores living for the benefit of others (a horizontal morality) and taking action for others that is motivated by love. This was James' concern.

> *If a brother or sister is without clothing and in need of daily food, and one of you says to them, "Go in peace, be warmed and be filled," and yet you do not give them what is necessary for their body, what use is that? Even so faith, if it has no works, is dead, being by itself.*
>
> James 2:15 – 17

Love is a choice to extend the action rightly attached to value. That is, an obligation where the vertical is extended to the horizontal.

The fourth insight is that the work of our salvation is 'how' we love others. 1 John 3:14 declares:

> *We know that we have passed out of death into life, because we love the brethren. He who does not love abides in death.*

We know that we have passed out of darkness into light, and we know we are born again by our love for others. The story of Zaccheus illustrates this trust:

> *Zaccheus stopped and said to the Lord, "Behold, Lord, half of my possessions I will give to the poor, and if I have defrauded anyone of anything, I will give back four times as much. And Jesus said to him, 'Today salvation has come to this house, because he, too, is a son of Abraham. For the Son of Man has come to seek and to save that which was lost.*
>
> Luke 19:8-10

How did Jesus know that salvation had come to Zaccheus? He knew because Zaccheus acted in love towards those he had previously stolen from. Zaccheus loved redemptively by restoring things to the way God created them to be.

Loving others is to be the centre of our spirituality from the day we are 'born again'.

The fifth insight is that when considering living righteously with one another, our mindsets and attitudes towards others are significant. Relational faithfulness is first and foremost about expressing loyalty and devotion to one another. It is not to be seen and acted upon as a way of conforming to a standard of behaviour out of fear of punishment. Nor is it for the sake of reward or merit.

> *Therefore if there is any encouragement in Christ, if there is any consolation of love, if there is any fellowship of the Spirit, if any affection and compassion, make my joy complete by being of the same mind, maintaining the same love, united in spirit, intent on one purpose. Do nothing from selfishness or empty conceit, but with humility of mind regard one another as more important than yourselves; do not merely look out for your own personal interests, but also for the interests of others. Have this attitude in yourselves which was also in Christ Jesus,*
>
> Phil. 2:1 – 5

Just as Jesus submitted Himself to us by giving His life for us, so we are to submit our interests to those of others. We are to put others first as Jesus put us first. For Paul, this is an obvious and logical application of Jesus' command to love one another as He has loved us.

CHAPTER 1

The sixth insight needs no commentary. It is pregnant with application. It stands head and shoulders above any other literary or philosophical discourse on love as well as being a definition of love. These verses can be viewed through the idea that love makes all things meaningful.

If I speak with the tongues of men and of angels, but do not have love, I have become a noisy gong or a clanging cymbal. If I have the gift of prophecy, and know all mysteries and all knowledge; and if I have all faith, so as to remove mountains, but do not have love, I am nothing. And if I give all my possessions to feed the poor, and if I surrender my body to be burned, but do not have love, it profits me nothing.

Love is patient, love is kind and is not jealous; love does not brag and is not arrogant, does not act unbecomingly; it does not seek its own, is not provoked, does not take into account a wrong suffered, does not rejoice in unrighteousness, but rejoices with the truth; bears all things, believes all things, hopes all things, endures all things.

Love never fails; but if there are gifts of prophecy, they will be done away; if there are tongues, they will cease; if there is knowledge, it will be done away. For we know in part and we prophesy in part; but when the perfect comes, the partial will be done away. When I was a child, I used to speak like a child, think like a child, reason like a child; when I became a man, I did away with childish things. For now we see in a mirror dimly, but then face to face; now I know in part, but then I will know fully just as I also have been fully known. But now faith, hope, love, abide these three; but the greatest of these is love.

1 Cor. 13: 1 – 13

> So, here they were, on a warm spring Saturday morning, hanging around in front of a decrepit weatherboard house, gardening tools in hand, waiting for the new guy to turn up. They could hear Mrs Sider coughing her lungs out inside. She'd once invited the boys into the house for a glass of water and afterwards they'd fallen about coughing and laughing and crying out 'It's Black Lung, Pop.' She had to be a smoker with a cough like that.
>
> 'Think that's him?' Ant said, nodding in the direction of a guy who was, at that moment, expertly mounting the curb with his skateboard. Ving gave a low whistle. A thousand thoughts collided in Red's mind as the new guy approached. A First Nations dude. Was this some kind of inclusion project on Dom's part?

The guy walked up to them carrying his skateboard under his arm. 'Lom,' he said, as he smiled at each of them in turn. Ant and Ving couldn't stop staring so Red had to make their introductions. Red was surprised to hear Lom spoke just like them. On television the indigenous actors all seem to have weird accents.

Red left the guys standing awkwardly together on the footpath and marched up to the front door. He grinned as he banged on the door. It took a while before the door creaked open and Mrs Sider's pale face appeared. 'Yes?' she rasped. She blinked rapidly in the bright summer light.

Red cleared his throat. 'Uh, Mrs Sider? We're here to…'

She nodded and closed the door.

'Can you believe this woman?' he said, hoping Mrs Sider would hear him. He walked back to the boys about to suggest they ditch this ingrate's house and go to the next job, only to see that Lom had already begun working on the garden beds. Ant and Ving looked at red questioningly. He jerked his head towards Lom. 'What's he trying to prove?'

Throughout the afternoon, Red watched in amazement as Lom expertly removed weeds, uncovering plants long hidden from sight. Each time he discovered a new plant, he invited the boys to enjoy it with him. 'This here's a rare Red-cross Spider-orchid,' Lom said, carefully exposing a spectacular crimson flower with a deep red centre. 'It only flowers for a few weeks every year.'

'How do you know all this stuff?' asked Red.

Lom tapped his heart. 'It's in my blood.'

'Yeah?' said Ving.

'The connection to land. Our people are born with it,' Lom said, with pride. Red liked the sound of that pride. He thought about his own family heritage. Was there anything to be proud of there? All he could remember were stories of dysfunction. Pretty depressing stuff.

Lom turned back to the flower. 'It's amazing to see one here. They're an endangered species.'

'Meaning?' asked Ving.

'It means they're on the brink of becoming extinct,' said Red.

'I wish the elderly were extinct,' said Ant, warming to his theme. 'Seriously, what are we doing here? The house is a pull-down job. The old lady will end up in a home. The weeds will take over again. It's a waste of our time.'

'Yeah, where are the hot girls who need the help of the Triple Threat?' said Ving, running his tongue over his lips.

'Need our help with what?' Red joked, grinning at Lom as he spoke. But instead of laughing, Lom remained silent. Red felt a wave of irritation. 'What's with you, Spider-flower man?' Red didn't know why he was trying to pick a fight with the new guy. All he knew was that Lom was different and Red didn't like different.

THE CALL TO COMMUNITY

The New Testament writers clearly presume that followers of Jesus are called to live in community. Equally, they recognised that living in community is messy! Admonish one another. Forgive one another. Be patient with one another. Stop passing judgement on one another. Don't bite and devour one another.

Jesus' call to follow Him included a call to live in community. Yet He built a community with people at different levels of spiritual experience, for example, Mary Magdalen compared to Peter and Andrew. He built with those who had a clash of cultural values, such as Matthew as a Tax Collector who supported the Roman oppressors and Simon the Zealot, a terrorist insurgent committed to overthrowing the Romans. He also built community in the midst of regular relational conflict, such as the claims of both James and John to be at the right and left hand of Jesus.

Jesus saw community as the powerhouse for learning how to love and serve others. He taught His followers to live with love as their centre-point, not power and control (Matt.20:24-28). He demonstrated the power of forgiveness (John 8:1-11) and instructed them on its importance (Matt.18:21-25). He warned against judgement of others (Matt.7:1-5). The New Testament commandment (John 13:34-35), to love one another, as I have loved you, can only be truly outworked in community life.

COMMUNITY: WHAT IS IT?

The Merriam-Webster dictionary[13] defines community broadly as: 'a unified body of individuals.' It further breaks down this broad idea into people with

---
13 x https://www.merriam-webster.com/dictionary/community?utm_campaign=sd&utm_medium=serp&utm_source=jsonld , accessed May 13th 2022

common interests: professional, social, economic, political, and, or policy orientated. They can live closely together within a larger society or be scattered throughout a larger society.

The original Greek word in the New Testament used for community is *koinonia*. It refers to fellowship, sharing, participation, and contribution.

In today's culture, the idea of community is understood in many different ways. Social media and digital connectivity are viewed as forming communities online. Activists for a cause generate a sense of tribalism and call it a community focused on a common enemy and will often disregard others. The identification with others through having similarities, based on the idea of 'a chemistry' amongst themselves, is also called community. Friendship and 'hang out' groups create a pseudo community that misses the depth of *koinonia*. They hold back on being fully known and transparent. Often these groups will fall into disarray when conflict emerges. Purpose-oriented group activity that pursues the same values within the same context of gathering is the most commonly recognised form of community. Focused small groups that gather for open dialogue that brings personal encouragement and support can be seen as an intimate community space.

The community that Jesus created with His followers was much deeper in its interactions and intent than most groups we would call community today. Community, as expressed through *koinonia*, was founded on a profound level of servanthood and commitment to the demands of living in right relationship with one another. It involves the pursuit of and willingness to being known and knowing others. It requires a focus on both hearing & understanding and being heard and understood. All of which assumes emotional and psychological openness and vulnerability. This experience of community seeks places and spaces that enable transformational experiences with the goal to live in and through the call to be like Jesus.

BARRIERS TO COMMUNITY

Followers of Jesus may hear and see the call of Jesus to this style of community. However, there are some barriers that are generally encountered in its pursuit.

The first barrier is the strong affiliation with the rights of self and individualism in our western culture. To live in *koinonia* requires a commitment to the authority of Jesus and Scripture. This authority requires the surrender of autonomy and knowing best. The need to surrender our lordship to His Lordship is magnified. Being self-centred and self-reliant are options that are challenged.

The second barrier is idealism. Most people love the idea of close, caring, and nurturing relationships. The reality, though, is that community is hard work. Idealism aspires to expectations that go unfulfilled. Often the expectations forget to acknowledge and account for the fact that we are all 'works in progress.' We all need transformation, and we all carry pain and brokenness.

Our pain comes from disappointments at best and abusive rejection at worst. We all live with areas of emotional deficit that need healing, and we look to others to remediate and soothe our pain. Community, at its best, promises such experiences and expectations. However, the reality of community is that it is a place of ongoing learning and discovery. It is a journey that offers endless destinations for growth, healing, and transformation.

The third barrier is a lack of understanding about how people think, lead and get things done across culture.

People from around the world see life in dramatically different ways. Erin Meyer in 'The Culture Gap'[14] has identified and describes eight scales showing how cultures vary along a spectrum.

Communicating
Low-context..High context

Evaluating
Direct negative feedback..................Indirect negative feedback

Persuading
Principles-first.......................................Applications-first

Leading
Egalitarian...Hierachical

Deciding
Consensual...Top-down

Trusting
Task-based..Relationship-based

Disagreeing
Confrontational......................................Avoids confrontation

Scheduling
Lineartime..Flexibletime

[14] Meyer, E., (2015), *The Culture Gap*, Public Affairs, a member of the Persus Books group

The Kingdom of God is a cross-cultural community. As such, there are any number of opportunities for misunderstandings that can arise from clashing cultural assumptions. There can be invisible barriers that need to be decoded through recognising the value any given culture gives to one of these scales. Understanding cultural biases, expectations and a view of life guards against ascribing intent and motives to others that informs tension and results in conflict.

The fourth barrier is fear and intimidation. To be genuinely heard and understood requires high levels of trust. However, trust can be easily lost when others respond from self-centredness, 'righteous' counsel, or insecurity. To be known and to know others requires the willingness for others to see our 'real self'. However, openness and vulnerability are frightening propositions when others are not familiar with the place of empathy. It is risky to believe that others won't judge who we are and are not.

This fear has its roots in Genesis 3. Judgement and sin entered the heart of mankind when Adam and Eve ate from the tree of the knowledge of good and evil.

> *Now they heard the sound of the Lord God walking in the garden in the cool of the day, and the man and his wife hid themselves from the presence of the Lord God among the trees of the garden. Then the Lord God called to the man, and said to him, "Where are you?" He said, "I heard the sound of You in the garden, and I was afraid because I was naked; so I hid myself."*
>
> Gen. 3:8-10

Sin causes us to hide, and we hide in our sin for fear and the shame of being judged. Yet the Lord's path to restoration is through community.

> *Therefore, confess your sins to one another, and pray for one another so that you may be healed. A prayer of a righteous person, when it is brought about, can accomplish much.*
>
> James 5:16

It is a righteous man whose prayers are answered. They that value, above all else, living in right standing and right relationship, whose prayers are answered.

IMPLICATIONS FOR COMMUNITY AND SPIRITUAL FORMATION

The call to love others is lived out as we pursue shalom: restoration that makes us whole and complete. It is also demonstrated as we practice, in community, our spirituality, the pursuit of restoration and love. Neuroscience, righteousness, and strong group culture provide us with real practical implications of the pursuits and practices of being radically restored to oneness with one another.

When considering the practical implications of neuroscience, Wilder and Hendricks[15] again provide some beneficial insights:

> Attachment is the strongest force in the human brain. It is not an emotion, although we feel it strongly, and attachment runs much deeper in the brain below wilful control. Attachment is the best word scientists could find for what glues people together and little creatures to their parents. It produces an enduring care for the well-being of another. Attachment is a life-giving forever bond with no mechanism in the brain to unglue us. If God has an enduring love for us that brings us good, the only force in the human brain that can understand such lasting kindness and care is the brain's attachment system. Joyful secure attachments build a good brain. Fearful or weak attachments build an identity centre that damages our relationships when we are upset. Character develops through relationships—that can handle times when things go wrong.

In the Old Testament the Hebrew word used to describe what the neuroscientists call attachment is *Hesed*. Wilder and Hendricks continue:

> Hesed is a kind and loyal care for the well-being of another. It carries the sense of an enduring connection that brings life and all good things into a relationship. Greek also has a word for the love that attaches all Christians to God and to one another, and that is *agape*, a very obscure Greek word until Christians started using it. When *Hesed* replaces truth as the foundation of discipleship, the whole model self-corrects. Placing love at the core of the transformation process allows truth, choice, and power to play their proper roles and not bear a weight they were never intended to carry... developments in modern brain science have made it clear that any model of transformation and character change must be anchored in the development of a love bond with God and His people.

The priority in pursuing this transformation is based on our love for others so that we do not contribute to the chaos of tension, anger, disappointment, and frustration in relationships. We pursue being whole and complete as an expression of our love for and devotion to Jesus.

---
15 Hendricks. M. and Wilder. J., (2020), Op. Cit. pg 80-85

When considering the practical implications of righteousness, the place of *Hesed* grows in significance. In His pursuit of being faithful to bring us into right standing and right relationship with Himself, God forms an *hesed* bond with us in Christ.

> *See how great a love the Father has given us, that we would be called children of God; and* **in fact** *we are. For this reason the world does not know us: because it did not know Him.*
>
> 1 John 3:1

So, we are joined to a spiritual family and community because of love.

John goes further in 1 John 4:7-9, 11-12 in declaring our loving attachment to our Father, Jesus, and each other gives us the clearest experience of the unseen God.

> *Beloved, let's love one another; for love is from God, and everyone who loves has been born of God and knows God. The one who does not love does not know God, because God is love. By this the love of God was revealed in us, that God has sent His only Son into the world so that we may live through Him.*
>
> *Beloved, if God so loved us, we also ought to love one another. No one has ever seen God; if we love one another, God remains in us, and His love is perfected in us.*

Hesed is the glue that binds us together as members of Jesus' family. When we fail to see our fellowship in the light of attachment, being members of one another, our views of the church become distorted.

Jesus' vision for the church is family. The way we live together is to be characterised by operating together in the following ways: we eat together; do life together; are loving and affectionate to one another; hold one another accountable through mercy, kindness, and grace; share resources and responsibilities; bear one another's burdens; make decisions together; release each other's destinies; and, are faithful to the relationship when conflict and tensions arise.

When considering the practical implications of a strong group culture of community, the key is found in maturing in our ability to relate. Being family is much more than a friendship group where you come and go as you please. The people who stay are the ones who grow. Genuine progress is pursuing shalom. Practising love is discovered in the crucible of long-term, interpersonal relationships.

CHAPTER 1

All long-term relationships in community face the following moments that, when navigated successfully, result in the experience of shalom. There is a honeymoon period where relational chemistry is enough to negotiate any negatives. Then there is familiarity, a taking for granted and apathy that can emerge when a lack of purposeful engagement drops away. The opportunity for conflict motivated by frustration and fear emerges and the work of remaining faithful to the relationship begins. Successfully negotiating these times results in a deeper acceptance and celebration of one another. We re-engage with a degree of idealism removed and move to a healthier and more whole version of ourselves. We'll look at this more later!

The truth is that family and communities with a strong group culture are the places of our deepest joys, hurts, and healings. Churches and communities with low attachment are generally looking to avoid the pain caused by deep attachment. Relationships in these communities function through transactional cultures based on performance; people remain acquaintances and therefore experience little separation pain. C.S. Lewis describes this avoidance of love and attachment in this way:

> To love at all is to be vulnerable. Love anything, and your heart will certainly be wrung and possibly be broken. If you want to make sure of keeping it intact, you must give your heart to no-one, not even to an animal. Wrap it carefully round with hobbies and little luxuries; avoid all entanglements; lock it up safe in the casket or coffin of your selfishness. But in that casket—safe, dark, motionless, airless—it will change. It will not be broken; it will become unbreakable, impenetrable, irredeemable.[16]

SUMMARY

— Our personal wholeness impacts how we pursue the practice of loving others.

— As we personally pursue being restored to the way God originally intended us to be, we sign up to a process of spiritual formation. That is, being more like Jesus in our daily lives.

— Neuroscience and neuropsychology are proving that effective spiritual formation requires activities that stimulate and develop the right side of the brain. They are also proving that we are 'soft wired' for sociability, attachment, affection, and companionship.

---

16 Lewis. C.S., (1960), *The Four Loves*, Harper Collins Publications. New York., Chapter 6 (accessed via eBook, therefore page number not provided)

— God's righteousness is His relentless willingness to forgive, reconcile and set right our relationship with Him. We must not confuse our right relationship with right standing in God.

— Jesus understands Christian community through a strong group culture framework of disciples who are pursuing doing the will of God.

— The understanding of the writers of the New Testament concerning righteousness and strong group culture has resulted in the emphasis on *allelon*.

— God's people are called to *Koinonia*, community that is based on deep levels of servanthood and commitment to the demands of being in right relationship with one another.

— Three barriers to community have been noted. The first is the strong affiliation with the rights of self and individualism in western culture. The second is idealism. The third is fear and intimidation.

— The practical implication of neuroscience and neuropsychology is how to develop attachment and bonds of love with God and His people.

— The practical implication of righteousness is that when we fail to see our fellowship in the light of attachment, being members of one another, our view of church community becomes distorted.

— The practical implication of a strong group culture of community is found in the maturing in our ability to relate.

QUESTIONS AND ACTIVITIES

1. What have you seen in the insights of neuroscience and neuropsychology that have influenced your spiritual formation journey?

2. Can yu identify two ways your relationship with God can be impacted through a Hebrew understanding of righteousness?

3. How would you begin to embrace a strong group culture in your pursuit of community?

4. What would you need to change to accept that while being right in your perspective, you can be wrong though acting unrighteously?

Chapter 2

A Call to Kingdom Relational Values

...Sharing the Divine Essence

- *Perichoresis,* the intimacy and reciprocity of the Trinity, is a divine dance we have been included in because of our righteousness.

- As partakers of the divine essence we are to release one another through relationships that are covenantal not contractural in nature.

- Expressing a commitment to being a people of discovery above conclusions will help to overcome division and disunity. Pursuing a lifestyle that establishes trust based relationships who are focused on restorative justice.

I am a shining example of the urban myth that white men can't dance. Yet dancing is a central feature of celebrations and community building in most human cultures.

If you have ever been to or seen footage of a Greek wedding, you will have seen a distinctive style of dancing. There are not two dancers, but at least three, sometimes many more. They begin by moving in circles weaving in and out in a fantastic pattern of motions. As the music continues, the pace picks up. The dancers' movements become faster and faster and faster, all the while staying in rhythm and sync with each other. Eventually, their individual identities and movements morph into one larger dance.

The Greek word *perichoresis* is the term that, over time, has been adopted and adapted by theologians to express the intimacy and reciprocity among the Persons of the Godhead. This intimacy and reciprocity has come to be referred to as the 'dance of love' into which all followers of Jesus are invited to take part. It is the one dance that I have given myself to discover and master. I want to be an answer to Jesus' prayer.

> *"I do not ask on behalf of these alone, but for those also who believe in Me through their word; that they may all be one; even as You, Father are in Me and I in You, that they may also be in Us, so that the world may believe that You sent Me".*

John 17:20-21

Perichoresis is seen in Jesus' prayer in John 17:1. "Father, the hour has come. Glorify Your Son, that Your Son may glorify You." We compare this with John 16:14, in which Jesus says that the Holy Spirit "will glorify Me". So, the Holy Spirit glorifies the Son, the Son glorifies the Father, and the Father glorifies the Son. The loving relationships within the Trinity result in the Persons of the Godhead giving glory to one another.

Perichoresis is the fellowship of three co-equal Persons perfectly embraced in love and harmony and expressing an intimacy that is difficult to comprehend. The Father sends the Son (John 3:16), and the Spirit proceeds from the Father and was sent by the Son (John 15:26) - another example of *perichoresis*, resulting in God's people being blessed.

Nothing separates the Persons of the Trinity or interrupts the mysterious interchange of *perichoresis*. It can be imagined as a Venn diagram showing three circles intersecting in the centre. Each circle intersects the others perfectly and multi-dimensionally as they rotate about a centre of divine love.[1]

Nathan Smith[2] describes *perichoresis* like this:

> From the beginning, God is Father, Son and Spirit, and from the beginning, this God has determined not to live without us. Before the blueprints for creation were drawn up, the Father, Son and Spirit set their abounding love upon us and determined that we would be adopted, that we would be given a place inside their circle of life, and made participants in the very fellowship and joy and glory of the Triune God. There and then, before creation, it was decided that the Son would cross every chasm between God and humanity and establish a real and abiding relationship - union. He was predestined to be the mediator, the one in and through whom the very life of the Triune God would enter human existence, and human existence would be lifted up to share in the Trinitarian life. The gospel is the good news that this stunning plan of the Triune God has now become eternal fact in Jesus Christ. In his incarnate life, death, resurrection and ascension, he laid hold of the human race, took us down in his death, recreated us in his resurrection, and lifted us up into the embrace of the Father in his ascension.

Perichoresis has come to represent the idea of a 'divine dance'. A dance between the Father, Son and Spirit and we as followers of Jesus have been brought into its fold. It describes a movement of love that has broken forth into our existence in Jesus Christ and has drawn all existence into the glorious yet mysterious divine. *Perichoresis* manifests the loving unity of the Trinity and the unconditional and incomprehensible love of God that disciples of Jesus are enveloped by and called to live in and out of.

> *Simon Peter, a bond servant and apostle of Jesus Christ, to those who have received a faith of the same kind as ours, by the righteousness of our God and Saviour, Jesus Christ: grace and peace be multiplied to you in the knowledge of God and of Jesus our Lord; seeing that His divine power has granted to us everything pertaining to life and godliness, through the true knowledge of Him who called us by His own glory and excellence. For by these He has granted to us His precious*

---

[1] Got Questions, (n.d.), *What is Perichoresis?*, Retrieved September 6th 2021 from https://www.gotquestions.org/perichoresis.html
[2] Music & Dancing, (2013), *The Dance of Love: perichoresis*, Retrieved from https://musicanddancing.wordpress.com/perichoresis/ on September 6th 2021

> *and magnificent promises, so that by them you may become partakers of the divine nature, having escaped the corruption that is in the world by lust.*
>
> 2 Peter 1:1-4

Perichoresis highlights the fact that the Trinity live in community. There are four characteristics and values of their community that empower the way followers of Jesus are called to live in oneness with each other.

Firstly, there is full equality. The Father and Son are one (John 10:30). The Holy Spirit proceeds from the Father (John 16:26), and He is like Jesus being with us forever (John 14:16).

Secondly, there is glad submission one to another. Jesus only says and does what He sees His Father doing (John 5:19-20), while the Holy Spirit speaks what He hears (John 16:13).

Thirdly, there is joyful intimacy. They bring glory to one another as they look to one another to serve those who love them (John 16:14-15).

Fourthly, there is mutual deference to one another (John 14:25-26).

Together, these characteristics and values result in reciprocal giving and receiving, expressions of unity and the essence of who one another are: mutual honour and respect, and collaborative effort. They are an open community, welcoming all who want to come and sit at their table. This is how they 'dance together'. They invite followers to mirror this invitation into a circle of love in their daily lives for themselves and others.

> *Now for this very reason also, applying all diligence, in your faith supply moral excellence, and in your moral excellence, knowledge, and in your knowledge self-control, perseverance, godliness, and in your godliness, brotherly kindness, love. For if these qualities are yours and are increasing, they render you neither useless nor unfruitful in the true knowledge of our Lord Jesus Christ. For he who lacks these qualities is blind or short sighted, having forgotten his purification from his former sins.*
>
> 2 Peter 1: 5-9

The call to apply diligence in faith, moral excellence, knowledge, self-control, perseverance, godliness, brotherly kindness and love is to grow in sharing the Trinity's divine essence while escaping corruption. There are then consequences. An increase in these qualities results in greater usefulness and fruitfulness due to a true knowledge of Jesus. A lack of these qualities results in being blind and short sighted, having forgotten how Jesus changed their life.

We are to share the Trinity's divine essence:

— as a fulfilment of Jesus' promise;

> *Jesus answered and said to him, "If anyone loves Me, he will keep My word; and My Father will love him, and We will come to him and make our abode with him."*
>
> John 14:23

— to be an answer to Jesus' prayer;

> *"I do not ask on behalf of these alone, but for those also who believe in Me through their word; that they may all be one; even as You, Father, are in Me and I in You, that they also may be in Us, so that the world may believe that You sent Me."*
>
> John 17:20-21

— and to live the life we are called to.

> *"for in Him we live and move and exist, as even some of your own poets have said, 'For we also are His children.' "Being then the children of God, we ought not to think that the Divine Nature is like gold or silver or stone, an image formed by the art and thought of man."*
>
> Acts 17:28-29

RIGHTEOUSNESS AND THE DIVINE ESSENCE

Righteousness has two sides. One side refers to our "right standing" with God because Jesus' atoning death paid for the penalty for sin. This has been the predominant emphasis of theological discussions and preaching for hundreds of years. The other side to righteousness is "right relationship". God's righteousness is expressed in His promised pursuit of re-establishing right relationship with mankind (Genesis 3:15). As partakers of God's divine nature, our righteous behaviour is focused on being in right relationship with God, ourselves and others.

Again, as previously noted, "Jesus saw that right relationships were the key to righteousness, rather than legalistically and dutifully acting out some prescribed behaviour."[3] So that which builds up and promotes unity is righteous. Whatever breaks down, degrades or divides a relationship is unrighteous. This understanding is illustrated by Paul when he writes:

> *And just as they did not see fit to acknowledge God any longer, God gave them over to a depraved mind, to do those things that are not proper, being filled with all unrighteousness, wickedness, greed, evil; full of envy, murder, strife, deceit, malice; they are gossips, slanderers, haters of God, insolent, arrogant, boastful, inventors of evil, disobedient to parents, without understanding, untrustworthy, unloving, unmerciful.*

> Romans 1:28-31

When you think about seeking first His righteousness (Matthew 6:33), what are you going to seek? As we have already received the forgiveness for all of our transgressions (Colossians 2:14; 2 Corinthians 5:19; Hebrews 10:11-12), to seek righteousness cannot be to seek right standing.

> *'Now where there is forgiveness of these things, there is no longer any offering for sin.'*

> Hebrews 10:18

To seek righteousness is to seek to be in right relationship with God and others, remembering that sin is more than falling short of rules and regulations. More fully, it is falling short of expressing love.

> *If you love Me, you will keep My commandments.*

> John 14:15

What does it look like practically to be one who seeks, hungers and thirsts for righteousness? Romans 12:9-17 provides a great starting point:

— let love be without hypocrisy

— abhor what is evil

— cling to what is good

— give preference to one another

---

3 Op. Cit, Faller (2017), Chapter 1 note ix

- contribute to the needs of the saints
- practise hospitality
- bless those who persecute you, curse not
- rejoice with those who rejoice
- weep with those who weep
- do not be haughty in mind
- do not be wise in your own estimation
- never pay back evil for evil to anyone
- overcome evil with good.

(We will explore this more in the next chapter.)

When we hold this more complete understanding of righteous and unrighteous behaviour, it places a different light on the following scriptures:

> *Therefore do not let what is for you a good thing be spoken of as evil; for the kingdom of God is not eating and drinking, but righteousness, peace and joy in the Holy Spirit. For he who in this way serves Christ is acceptable to God and approved by men.*
>
> Romans 14:16-18
>
> *But seek first His kingdom and His righteousness, and all these things will be added to you.*
>
> Matthew 6:33
>
> *Little children, make sure no one deceives you; the one who practices righteousness is righteous, just as He is righteous; the one who practices sin is of the devil; for the devil has been sinning from the beginning. The Son of God appeared for this purpose, to destroy the works of the devil.*
>
> 1 John 3:7-8
>
> *Blessed are those who hunger and thirst for righteousness, for they will be satisfied.*
>
> Matthew 5:6

Kingdom living is not simply a matter of ethical adherence or following the rules. As Paul put it, it is not "eating and drinking". It is not a righteousness achieved through correct behavioural performance as set out in the Law.

> '...because by the works of the Law no flesh will be justified in His sight; ...but now apart from the Law the righteousness of God has been manifested, ...even the righteousness of God through faith in Jesus Christ.'
>
> Romans 3:20,21,22

Kingdom living is a matter of becoming a partaker of the divine nature because:

> "He who knew no sin, became sin on my behalf, that we might become the righteousness of God in Him".
>
> 2 Corinthians 5:21

I am righteous, being 'holy and blameless and beyond reproach' (Colossians 1:22). So now I am living in the Kingdom as I live like Jesus by fulfilling the mandate of being in right relationship with all men:

> "If possible, as far as it depends on you, be at peace with all men."
>
> Romans 12:18

Paul makes it clear that when we serve Christ in THIS way, focused on sharing the divine essence with others through what we have received, righteousness, peace and joy, we are acceptable to God and approved by men. Why?

> So then we pursue the things which make for peace and the building up of one another.
>
> Romans 14:19

CONTRACT AND COVENANT

Christopher Marshall expounds on righteousness as the relational working out of just relations:

> The biblical notion of righteousness refers broadly to doing, being, declaring or bringing about what is right. Righteousness is a comprehensively relational reality. It is not a private moral attribute as one has on one's own. It is something that inheres in our relationships as social beings. To be righteous is to be true to the demands of a rela-

tionship, whether that relationship is with God or with other persons.[4]

A key 'demand of a relationship' when loving one another as Jesus loved us (John 13:34) is to abstain from judgement. Greg Boyd begins his book 'Repenting of Religion' by observing:

> We love insofar as we abstain from judgement. Love is the central command in Scripture and judgement the central prohibition.[5]

In the first book in this series, 'Radically Restored to Oneness with God', I took more time to consider the place of judgement in undermining our pursuit of oneness with God and with others. My thoughts included:

> God's original intent, as evidenced by having two trees in the garden is that we would partake of His life, the tree of life. We are to surrender our lordship by not eating from the tree of the knowledge of good and evil. Before coming to put our trust in Jesus, we centre our lordship on making our own judgements. These are based on thoughts and decisions that are primarily focused on benefiting us. We discover how to rely on ourselves rather than relying on the Lord's all knowing insights and judgements, thus creating personal and ethnic cultures anchored in judgement.

> Where acceptance was freely given by God to Adam and Eve as an expression of oneness, the exchange to knowing good from evil resulted in finding acceptance through the evaluating filter of good and evil. We receive and acquire acceptance, worth and value on the condition that our knowledge of good and evil approves of behaviour. Acceptance is found in performance where we strive to display and acquire all that we deem good, and we desire to suppress and avoid all we consider evil.

> We see this in Adam and Eve when their eyes of judgement were opened: fear (hiding from God), shame and condemnation (covering their nakedness), and blame and accusation (defending themselves) dominated how they now related to God, self and others. They moved from a relationship with God and others with acceptance at its core to a relationship with Satan with judgement based on performance at their core.

---

4 Marshall, C., (2012), *Divine Justice as Restorative Justice*. Retrieved from http://www.baylor.edu/content/services/document.php/163072.pdf on September 6th 2021
5 Boyd, G., Op.cit., pg 9

The nature of Satan as a father is to make false judgements about everything. "Whenever he speaks a lie, he speaks from his own nature, for he is a liar and the father of lies." (John 8:44) He is the father of lies and judgement because he conceived of judgement in himself when he judged he was better than God.

How you have fallen from heaven,
O star of the morning, son of the dawn!
You have been cut down to the earth,
You who have weakened the nations!
"But you said in your heart,
'I will ascend to heaven;
I will raise my throne above the stars of God,
And I will sit on the mount of assembly
In the recesses of the north.
I will ascend above the heights of the clouds;
I will make myself like the Most High.'

    Isaiah 14:12-14

We were created to live in covenant relationship with God. A covenant is a formal agreement between two or more persons to do or not do something specified. A covenant is entered voluntarily and is accompanied by giving an oath that binds one party to the other with obligations. Genesis 2:15-17 is God's invitation to Adam to live in covenant relationship with Him:

Then the Lord took the man and put him in the garden of Eden to cultivate it and keep it. For the Lord God commanded the man, saying, "From any tree of the garden you may eat freely, but from the tree of the knowledge of good and evil you shall not eat, for in the day you eat from it you will surely die."

As federal representatives of mankind, when Adam and Eve ate of the tree of the knowledge of good and evil, they both broke covenant with God and reaped the capacity to make inadequate judgements. One of the greatest inadequacies is our propensity to judge others based on their performance.

It is in this context that Jesus simply said: "Judge not, so that you will not be judged" (Matthew 7:1). The Greek word here implies: 'to press harsh judgement'. When we judge others' performance harshly, we act from a place of 'inner consent' with our standards, expectations, or beliefs. However, in discipling relationships, theological conversations and leadership decision making, there is an appropriate place for critical thinking and commentary that is helpful, not harsh and destructive.

> *For in the way you judge, you will be judged; and by your standard of measure, it will be measured to you. Why do you look at the speck that is in your brother's eye, but do not notice the log that is in your own eye? Or how can you say to your brother, 'Let me take the speck out of your eye,' and behold, the log is in your own eye? You hypocrite, first take the log out of your own eye, and then you will see clearly to take the speck out of your brother's eye.*
>
> Matthew 7:2-5

This posture leads to being humble and motivated toward offering grace and mercy over judgement (James 2:13).

Mercy is defined as: extending compassion to an offender or refraining from enforcing what is due. God's very nature and being is merciful, as shown in Exodus 34:6-7.

> *Then the Lord passed by in front of him and proclaimed, "The Lord, the Lord God, compassionate and gracious, slow to anger, and abounding in lovingkindness and truth; who keeps lovingkindness for thousands, who forgives iniquity, transgression and sin, yet He will by no means leave the guilty unpunished, visiting the iniquity of fathers on the children and on the grandchildren to the third and fourth generations."*

God has determined to be merciful before sin and wrongdoing have taken place. Jesus calls us to be merciful, even as your Father is merciful (Luke 6:36). We are to clothe ourselves in tender-hearted mercy (Colossians 3:12). God's mercy is new every morning (Lamentations 3:22).

Mercy is the engine room for God to pursue right relationship with all. Jonah knew this to be true of God. He avoided doing the will of God because he wanted Nineveh to be judged.

> *But it greatly displeased Jonah and he became angry. He prayed to the Lord and said, "Please Lord, was not this what I said while I was still in my **own** country? Therefore, in order to forestall this I fled to Tarshish, for I knew that You are a gracious and compassionate God, slow to anger and abundant in lovingkindness, and one who relents concerning calamity. Therefore now, O Lord, please take my life from me, for death is better to me than life." The Lord said, "Do you have a good reason to be angry?"*

Jonah 4:1-4

I wonder whether God's people struggle to live in oneness with others because they prefer to be more like Jonah than God?

> *Then God said to Jonah, "Do you have good reason to be angry about the plant?" And he said, "I have good reason to be angry, even to death." Then the Lord said, "You had compassion on the plant for which you did not work and which you did not cause to grow, which came up overnight and perished overnight. Should I not have compassion on Nineveh, the great city in which there are more than 120,000 persons who do not know the difference between their right and left hand, as well as many animals?"*

Jonah 4:9-11

In contrast to a covenant, a contract is an agreement between the parties that creates mutual obligations based on performance. A contract outlines the expectations and is designed to protect the parties if the expectations are not met. The protections in a contract are formed around the capacity to punish the party that does not perform and to seek restitution and/or retribution.

The Kingdom of God relies on covenant relationships as expressed by *perichoresis* and maintained by righteousness. When the Adamic covenant as set out in Genesis 2:15-17 was broken, God expressed His desire to re-establish a relationship of joyful intimacy (acceptance) and His willingness to remain faithful to the relationship with mankind when He declared:

> *Then the Lord God said to the serpent,*
> *"Because you have done this,*
> *Cursed are you more than all the livestock,*
> *And more than any animal of the field;*
> *On your belly you shall go,*
> *And dust you shall eat*
> *All the days of your life;*
> *And I will make enemies*
> *Of you and the woman,*
> *And of your offspring and her Descendant;*
> *He shall bruise you on the head,*
> *And you shall bruise Him on the heel."*

Genesis 3:14-15

Jesus, the second Adam, through His sinless life, death and resurrection, has established a new covenant.

> *For since by a man death **came**, by a man also **came** the resurrection of the dead. For as in Adam all die, so also in Christ all will be made alive.*
>
> *So also it is written: "The first man, Adam, became a living person." The last Adam **was** a life-giving spirit. However, the spiritual is not first, but the natural; then the spiritual. The first man is from the earth, earthy; the second man is from heaven. As is the earthy one, so also are those who are earthy; and as is the heavenly one, so also are those who are heavenly. Just as we have borne the image of the earthly, we will also bear the image of the heavenly.*
>
> 1 Corinthians 15:21-22; 45-49
>
> *For this reason He is the mediator of a new covenant, so that, since a death has taken place for the redemption of the violations that were **committed** under the first covenant, those who have been called may receive the promise of the eternal inheritance.*
>
> Hebrews 9:15

To show ourselves to be sons of God or children of God, we must learn to live with an attitude of covenant toward all people and abandon any sense of contract.

> *But I say to you, love your enemies and pray for those who persecute you, so that you may prove yourselves to be sons of your Father who is in heaven; ... Therefore you shall be perfect, as your heavenly Father is perfect.*
>
> Matthew 5:44,45(a), 48

We live in contract with each other when, after judging that their behaviour is unsatisfactory according to our "knowledge of good and evil" (right and wrong), we permit ourselves to, at a minimum, judge them and, at worst, attack them.

In contrast, a covenantal attitude to relationships results in being committed to remaining in a peaceful and harmonious relationship with all, including our enemies and those who persecute us. We can offer commentary and observation about people's behaviour that is not critical or judgemental. We live by the principle that "tension doesn't mean something is wrong; it means something is happening." We can agree to disagree by playing the ball and not the man. We can engage in an exchange of ideas and perspectives without judging the intent and motive or being critical of the person involved. So many relationships break down because people live with the attitude of contract, not covenant.

I have only one formal covenant relationship with another person, and that is with my wife, Lyn. I am *not* advocating that we set up binding relationships with others outside of marriage. I am, however, advocating that we adopt the attitude and posture of covenant with all people. I am committed to a lifestyle of self-awareness and personal responsibility so that I address my contribution to any chaos or tension in my relationships. Paul's comments are again helpful:

> *Therefore do not go on passing judgment before* **the** *time,* **but wait** *until the Lord comes, who will both bring to light the things hidden in the darkness and disclose the motives of* **human** *hearts; and then praise will come to each person from God.*
>
> 1 Corinthians 4:5

Sharing the divine essence through Kingdom relational values appears to be always at the forefront of Paul's understanding of how God's people are to live together. As a reminder, let's again ponder that Paul wrote the following after clearly stating that our calling in life is to know our oneness with God so that we can live in oneness with one another.

> *Therefore I, the prisoner of the Lord, urge you to walk in a manner worthy of the calling with which you have been called, with all humility and gentleness, with patience, bearing with one another in love, being diligent to keep the unity of the Spirit in the bond of peace.* ***There is*** *one body and one Spirit, just as you also were called in one hope of your calling; one Lord, one faith, one baptism, one God and Father of all who is over all and through all and in all.*
>
> Ephesians 4:1-6

Paul talks again about the importance of oneness with each other in his writings to the Corinthians:

> *On the contrary, it is much truer that the parts of the body which seem to be weaker are necessary; and those parts of the body which we consider less honourable, on these we bestow greater honour, and our less*

> *presentable parts become much more presentable, whereas our more presentable parts have no need of it. But God has so composed the body, giving more abundant honour to that part which lacked, so that there may be no [division in the body, but that the parts may have the same care for one another. And if one part of the body suffers, all the parts suffer with it; if a part is honoured, all the parts rejoice with it.*
>
> 1 Corinthians 12:22-26

Of course, when I bring out these truths, some will object by quoting the need to tell others "the truth in love." When people try and justify behaviour that represents a contractual posture in relationship with this statement, my question in return is: "Whose truth are you wanting to tell them?" Always remember that truth is first and foremost a person: "I am the way, the truth and the life." (John 14:6)

Jesus only diverged from words that were compassionate, forgiving and accepting of tax collectors, prostitutes and ordinary sinners when He challenged the religious leaders' interpretation of the truth. Greg Boyd's thoughts are again helpful:

> Why is this? Didn't Jesus love the Pharisees, scribes, and Sadducees? Of course he did. Jesus loved them as much as any other sinners. In fact, even while he publicly confronted them, his heart broke for them as well as for those they were harming. On one occasion, he concluded his harsh confrontation of religious leaders by crying out "O Jerusalem, Jerusalem, you who kill the prophets and stone those sent to you, how often I have longed to gather your children together, as a hen gathers her chicks under her wings, but you were not willing" (Matt.23:37). We see that Jesus wanted to gather these blind leaders and their followers under his protection! Knowing that these leaders would put him to death within days, Jesus still expressed the loving, longing and forgiving heart of God for them. And even after they crucified him, Jesus prayed for their forgiveness (Luke 23:34)
>
> Why then, were Jesus' words to and about these religious leaders so harsh? The answer is that they *had to be*. Whereas love usually requires we affirm worth by showing compassion toward people, in certain cases it requires aggressive confrontation. If a person is in a severe state of blindness and hardness of heart, and especially if a person is in a leadership position and is damaging to others

with his or her blindness and hardness, intervention may be necessary. Families or groups of friends who have had to deal with loved ones addicted to alcohol, drugs, or pornography know this side of love well. Such was the case with certain religious leaders of Jesus' day. These leaders were in grave danger and were placing others in grave danger. A radical intervention was called for.

We have addressed the church's need to embody Jesus' outrageous love toward all people. But how are we to apply Jesus' confrontation of harmful religious leaders today? Some have mistakenly taken Jesus' confrontation of the Pharisees, scribes, and Sadducees as a justification for overtly confronting sin *wherever* they see it (except in themselves), whether inside or outside the church.[6]

When we permit ourselves to live in contract with others, we are living through the consequences of the first Adam eating from the tree of the knowledge of good and evil. From this place, we cannot live a life based on *perichoresis*, righteousness and covenant. Living from a 'contractual attitude' towards our relationships is so often at the centre of the division and disunity that so often exists in the body of Christ. This is my next focus.

However, in the next chapter, I will attempt to draw on my experience to illustrate practical ways to be diligent in preserving the bonds of peace and unity. In Chapter 4, we will consider the place of personal transformation to empower our hearts to live in an attitude of covenant.

> Lom stood up and brushed the dirt from his hands onto his shorts. 'What's happening here, Red?' he asked, quietly. 'Have I offended you?'
>
> Red knew he'd backed himself into a corner and would have to fight his way out. He couldn't back down. 'Look, us guys,' he said, indicating Ant and Ving who at that moment were looking at Red with undisguised interest, 'have grown up together. We're like the same person. We're not used to having a fourth man.'
>
> Lom raised his eyebrows. 'A fourth man like me?'
>
> Listen, buddy, I'm not racist. You people can chant on the land all you want. I'm just saying that your way isn't our way.' Red knew he was being offensive. But he was having trouble controlling his words.

---

6   Boyd, G., (2004)., *Repenting of Religion: Turning from Judgement to the Love of God*. Baker Books Michigan pg 202,203.

'Help me understand where you're coming from, Red,' said Lom.

A guttural cough coming from the side of the house arrested the conversation. Mrs Sider was making her way slowly towards them carrying a tray of iced water and a plate of something that looked like brownies. The 'fresh-out-of-the-oven' smell as she got closer made Red's mouth water. He groaned. Burning coals were being heaped on his head.

'I just wanted…to say…thank you,' said Mrs Sider, in a breathless voice. A paroxysm of coughing followed. It was the first time Red had seen her in the light and was shocked at how thin her body was. 'I've…been watch…watching…you all…from …the window and…you,' she said turning to Lom, 'you…most of all…have been…bringing my garden…its beauty…back to how…it used…to be.'

DIVISION AND DISUNITY

When a 'contractual attitude' to relationships is adopted, the focus quickly gravitates to proving right and wrong, proving what is appropriate or inappropriate. Tension and conflict are defined by the discovery of what or who is wrong. Having established what is wrong, the next step is finding a way to bring correction that often involves punishment or retaliation.

This is how the Pharisees and Sadducees approached their relationship to Jesus, and how they approached sin through an interpretation of what was good and what was evil. This interpretation resulted in assessing Jesus from a starting point of judging His behaviour as wrong. From where the Pharisees and Sadducees stood, Jesus broke a long list of rules:

Jesus was attended to by women who had been prostitutes.

> *And there was a woman in the city who was a sinner; and when she learned that He was reclining* **at the table** *in the Pharisee's house, she brought an alabaster vial of perfume, and standing behind* **Him** *at His feet, weeping, she began to wet His feet with her tears, and she wiped them with the hair of her head, and* **began** *kissing His feet and anointing them with the perfume. Now when the Pharisee who had invited Him saw* **this**, *he said to himself, "If this man were a prophet He would know who and what sort of person this woman* **is** *who is touching Him, that she is a sinner!"*

Luke 7:37-39

He fellowshipped with tax collectors, drunkards and sinners.

> *And Levi gave a big reception for Him in his house; and there was a large crowd of tax collectors and other **people** who were reclining **at the table** with them. The Pharisees and their scribes **began** grumbling to His disciples, saying, "Why do you eat and drink with the tax collectors and sinners?"*
>
> Luke 5:29-30

He healed and fellowshipped with lepers.

> *And a man with leprosy came to Jesus, imploring Him and kneeling down, and saying to Him, "If You are willing, You can make me clean." Moved with compassion, **Jesus** reached out with His hand and touched him, and said to him, "I am willing; be cleansed." And immediately the leprosy left him, and he was cleansed.*
>
> Mark 1:40-42

He didn't require His disciples to fast.

> *John's disciples and the Pharisees were fasting; and they came and said to Him, "Why do John's disciples and the disciples of the Pharisees fast, but Your disciples do not fast?" And Jesus said to them, "While the groom is with them, the attendants of the groom cannot fast, can they? As long as they have the groom with them, they cannot fast. But the days will come when the groom is taken away from them, and then they will fast, on that day.*
>
> Mark 2:18-20

Jesus contradicted respected Jewish leaders.

> *But wanting to justify himself, he said to Jesus, "And who is my neighbour? Jesus replied and said, "A man was going down from Jerusalem to Jericho, and he encountered robbers, and they stripped him and [a]beat him, and went away leaving him half dead. And by coincidence a priest was going down on that road, and when he saw him, he passed by on the other side. Likewise a Levite also, when he came to the place and saw him, passed by on the other side. But a Samaritan who was on a journey came upon him; and when he saw him, he felt compassion, and came to him and bandaged up his wounds,*

> *pouring oil and wine on **them**; and he put him on his own animal, and brought him to an inn and took care of him. On the next day he took out two denarii and gave them to the innkeeper and said, 'Take care of him; and whatever more you spend, when I return, I will repay you.' Which of these three do you think proved to be a neighbour to the man who fell into the robbers' **hands?**" And he said, "The one who showed compassion to him." Then Jesus said to him, "Go and do the same."*

Luke 10:29-37

Jesus healed on the Sabbath.

> *As he was passing through a field of grain on the sabbath, his disciples began to make a path while picking the heads of grain. At this the Pharisees said to him, "Look, why are they doing what is unlawful on the sabbath?"*

Mark 2:23-24

For these reasons and more, they wanted retributive justice and settled on having Him killed (John 11:47-53).

When we begin to relate to others from the framework of broken expectations and a contractual attitude, we are getting life from what we are against. This is defined by our own self-serving version of the knowledge of good and evil. If love is the centre of life in God's Kingdom, then a contractual attitude moves us to the perimeter and beyond. On the perimeter, people often permit themselves to pursue their sense of justice in criticism at best and through marginalising and punishment of those they feel wronged by at worst.

Jesus' vision of the Kingdom is to invite people into the New Covenant, which is a new way of being in relationship with God and each other. This way of love recognises justice as the restoration of peace in relationships, not the pain of punishment.

> *Until the Spirit is poured out upon us from on high,*
> *And the wilderness becomes a fertile field,*
> *And the fertile field is considered as a forest.*
> *Then justice will dwell in the wilderness,*
> *And righteousness will remain in the fertile field.*
> *And the work of righteousness will be peace,*
> *And the service of righteousness, quietness and [a]confidence forever.*

> *Then my people will live in a peaceful settlement,*
> *In secure dwellings, and in undisturbed resting places;*

Isaiah 32:15-18

Christopher Marshall again provides helpful insights here:

> The restorative power of biblical justice is also evident at *the macro level* in the overall direction of the canonical story. The biblical meta-narrative can be read as one large story of God's restorative justice at work. God creates a perfect, harmonious world, one in which everything is as it ought to be, where human beings live in right relationship with one another, with God, and with the wider created order.
>
> But humankind violates these relationships. In a sense, humanity commits a crime against God, and inherits the damaging and enslaving consequences of doing so (cf. Romans 5:12-21). It is a crime against God's love as much as against God's law (Genesis 3:8-9). Adam and Eve are expelled from the Garden: they are alienated from relationship with God, with each other, and with the very ground of their origin (Genesis 3:22-24).
>
> But God, the righteous judge (Genesis 18:25; Romans 3:5-6), sets in motion the long historical process of recovery. God undertakes to do all that is necessary to restore humanity to its rightful place in creation and to repair the damage inflicted.[7]

It is evident that New Testament Christian communities were endeavouring to shape themselves through their experience of God's restorative justice in Jesus. Galatians 6:1 reveals a desire to normalise the restoration of sinners, not to bring harsh rejection and punishment.

> *Brothers, even if a person is caught in some transgression, you who are spiritual should correct that one in a gentle spirit, looking to yourself, so that you also may not be tempted.*

Where harsh punishment has been pursued, there is genuine concern that a punitive response does not have the last say:

> *Sufficient for such a person is this punishment which* **was imposed** *by the majority, so that on the other hand, you should rather forgive*

---

[7] Marshall. C., (2012)., *Divine Justice as Restorative Justice*. Centre for Christian Ethics pg 16

> *and comfort **him**, otherwise such a person might be overwhelmed by excessive sorrow. Therefore I urge you to reaffirm **your** love for him.*
>
> *But one whom you forgive anything, I also **forgive**; for indeed what I have forgiven, if I have forgiven anything, **I did** so for your sakes in the presence of Christ, so that no advantage would be taken of us by Satan, for we are not ignorant of his schemes.*
>
> 2 Corinthians 2:6-8; 10-11

Where a penalty has created a 'godly grief that produces repentance', the time for forgiveness and consolation has come to mitigate against grief and shame. God's justice desires liberation and restoration because it is centred in love.

David McHugh explores these ideas concerning the pursuit of the matters we call social justice:

> Over the past few years, I have witnessed the church increase its public engagement in what would be considered 'issues of justice'. Recently, in Australia, there have been many heated social debates whereby the church has publicly weighed in on the justice issues being debated. Issues such as immigration, abortion, and the legalisation of same-sex marriage. However, a poor theology of justice has been displayed in the way much of the church has engaged in these conversations. Within the church, rather than justice being about the restoration of relationship, bearing witness to the Kingdom of God and living towards a vision of shalom, the pursuit of justice has become about 'right and wrong' and taking a particular side on an issue. In these conversations, the church has had, not only a divided voice but a divisive posture toward those within the church who hold differing opinions and perspectives. In many cases, the public hostility has been justified as it is part of advocating for an 'issue of justice'. Brothers and sisters in Christ have become enemies, and the church currently reflects the "divisions and contradictions of the world."
>
> There ought to be a great concern for the dividedness that is sweeping across the church, all in the name of 'justice'. This division is the very antithesis of God's redemptive, restorative and reconciling justice, as well as what it means to live justly. The church argues, fights and dehumanises one another on these issues in the public arena when we are meant to be known by the world as His disciples because of our love for one another (John 13:34-35). It is a sad

reality and a "flagrant betrayal of Christian unity when children of the same Father, disciples of the same Lord, at a word from their secular rulers take up arms against one another..." It is the will of the Father that His followers are one and unified. In John 17:21, we read a segment of what is known as the High Priestly prayer or the Farewell prayer. A prayer where Jesus prays that we, the body of Christ might be one so that the world would believe in Him. Despite the repeated call for unity and the plea to pursue oneness, it is not difficult to see that the church is divided. Unfortunately, the reality of division has been significantly highlighted in the public sphere when it comes to issues of justice'.

In a world of growing polarisation and divergent values, both within the church and society at large, when the church's pursuit of justice fails to seek first the kingdom, further division is caused. Rather than the church playing its part in bearing witness to the kingdom of God and mending the fabric of shalom, it is actively involved in the perpetuation of disunity and disharmony. It is essential to recognise that to be unified, and one with one another does not equate to sameness and total agreement. For example, I have never met an individual that I agree with on absolutely everything all of the time. Therefore, it is unrealistic for people to expect the universal church to reach agreement on all issues confronting humanity. However, despite experiencing disagreement with someone, I can maintain a heart posture and commitment to unity and oneness.

Until the church can learn to live justly amongst one another, how can it expect to pursue justice within society? Biblical justice is primarily about the restoration of broken relationships. Love itself became justice when Jesus died on the cross and restored humanity into a right relationship with God. The impact of the fall is evident all around us. Division is everywhere. However, the church is unable to authentically pursue justice if it is not willing to embrace the fullness of shalom among one another. The church cannot accomplish its mission by skilfully piecing together its divided nature. A commonality in mission and shared vision is required to unify the body.

The church is called to seek *first* the kingdom of God and with that as the unifying framework to pursue righteousness and justice. Understanding and pursuing *justice*- the setting of things right - in light and reference to the kingdom of God will enable the church to recognise that the posture in the pursuit of justice is just as critical as the pursuit itself. A new understanding of justice is required. An understanding that takes into consideration the purpose that justice has in bearing witness to the kingdom of God, whereby the primary manifestation of the kingdom is shalom. God's mission is the establishment of His kingdom and the vision of the kingdom is shalom. In this way, shalom is not only the desired end but also the required means, as the church seeks first God's kingdom and His righteousness and justice.[8]

Marshall continues to help us consider these ideas when he writes:

> Justice in Israel involved doing all that was needed to create, sustain and restore healthy relationships within the covenantal community. Criminal offending was considered wrong, first, because it breaches the relational commitments that hold society together, and second, because the wrongful deeds themselves unleash a disordering power in the community that threatens to trigger a chain reaction of ruin and disaster unless it was arrested.
>
> One way of arresting this negative power, especially in situations of very grave interpersonal and religious offending, was by redirecting the destructive consequences of the deed back on the perpetrator by way of judicial or divine retribution. The punishment served simultaneously to dramatise the catastrophic consequences of evil deeds and to "purge the evil from Israel" (Deuteronomy 17:12). When this happened, justice was vindicated, not be the act of retributive punishment per se, but by the fact that the community had been delivered and restored to wholeness.[9]

Division and disunity are the predictable fruit of a contractual attitude to relationships. Here relationships are transactional in nature to achieve an outcome. The outcome is inevitably tied to upholding a predetermined position based on broken expectations. This is the antithesis of creating, sustaining and restoring healthy relationships within a covenant framework of relationships. That is, oneness with others.

In a contractual framework, the approach to relational tension is inevitably to 'prosecute a cause'. The starting point for this prosecution is one person or group's conclusion of how another person or group is wrong, and they are

---

8 McHugh. D., (2019) *Research Thesis*, Kilns College pg 2-4
9 Marshall. C., Op. Cit. pg 14

right. In stark contrast, Jesus approached relational tension through process and conversations of discovery.

> *But Jesus went to the Mount of Olives. And early in the morning He came again into the temple **area**, and all the people were coming to Him; and He sat down and **began** teaching them. Now the scribes and the Pharisees brought a woman caught in the act of adultery, and after placing her in the centre **of the courtyard**, they said to Him, "Teacher, this woman has been caught in the very act of committing adultery. Now in the Law, Moses commanded us to stone such women; what then do You say?" Now they were saying this to test Him, so that they might have **grounds for** accusing Him. But Jesus stooped down and with His finger wrote on the ground. When they persisted in asking Him, He straightened up and said to them, "He who is without sin among you, let him **be the** first to throw a stone at her." And again He stooped down and wrote on the ground.*

> John 8:1-11

Approaching relational dynamics from a predetermined conclusion results in proving points at the expense of another. This is the fruit of being illegitimately enthroned as judge through the tree of the knowledge of good and evil. Invariably the prosecutor, in a community setting, establishes allies, called the 'good guys'. This is to make sure those aligned with the prosecuted, the 'bad guys', are defeated. In this process, the intent and motive of the prosecuted are assumed, often wrongly. These assumptions fortify and embolden the determination of the prosecutors to be right.

JESUS' INVITATION

Often when Jesus was invited into conversations where others had predetermined conclusions, he was not looking for a debate or to be right.

> *When Jesus had finished these words, He left Galilee and came into the region of Judea beyond the Jordan; and large crowds followed Him, and He healed them there.*

> *Some Pharisees came to Jesus, testing Him and asking, "Is it lawful **for a man** to divorce his wife for any reason **at all?**" And He answered and said, "Have you not read that He who created **them** from the beginning made them male and female, and said, 'For this reason a man shall leave his father and his mother and be joined to his wife, and the*

> *two shall become one flesh'? So they are no longer two, but one flesh. Therefore, what God has joined together, no person is to separate." They said to Him, "Why, then, did Moses command to give **her** a certificate of divorce and send her away?" He said to them, "Because of your hardness of heart Moses permitted you to divorce your wives; but from the beginning it has not been this way. And I say to you, whoever divorces his wife, except for sexual immorality, and marries another woman commits adultery]."*
>
> *The disciples said to Him, "If the relationship of the man with his wife is like this, it is better not to marry." But He said to them, "Not all men **can** accept this statement, but **only** those to whom it has been given.*

Matthew 19:1-11

Jesus had a very clear and uncompromising perspective on divorce: "and I say to you whoever divorces his wife, except for immorality, and marries another woman commits adultery." The disciples understood the strength of Jesus' position and concluded, "It is better not to marry". Jesus didn't jump on this and declare, "You are right." Neither did He denigrate other perspectives. In fact, He was very sanguine when He acknowledged that some would agree and others would disagree with Him. That appears to be okay for Jesus because being right was always subservient to enjoying discovery based on love and respect.

Jesus made this approach to what He has to say very clear when He said:

> *If anyone hears My teachings and does not keep them, I do not judge him; for I did not come to judge the world, but to save the world. The one who rejects Me and does not accept My teachings has one who judges him: the word which I spoke. That will judge him on the last day.*

John 12:47-48

Here Jesus is pointing to the principles of permission and responsibility. That is, we have a free will. We get to choose what permission we give ourselves to accept or not accept what He has said. However, the permission we take and give ourselves places us in a position of accountability and responsibility for the subsequent behaviour.

To be an answer to Jesus' prayer and seek being one with another for the sake of the gospel is not a unique challenge for the church today. Differences of opinion or perspective associated with anger and point-scoring were a challenge in New Testament times too.

> You know *this*, my beloved brothers *and sisters*. Now everyone must be quick to hear, slow to speak, *and* slow to anger; for a man's anger does not bring about the righteousness of God. Therefore, ridding *yourselves* of all filthiness and *all* that remains of wickedness, in humility receive the word implanted, which is able to save your souls. But prove yourselves doers of the word, and not just hearers who deceive themselves. For if anyone is a hearer of the word and not a doer, he is like a man who looks at his natural face in a mirror; for *once* he has looked at himself and gone away, he has immediately forgotten what kind of person he was. But one who has looked intently at the perfect law, the *law* of freedom, and has continued *in it*, not having become a forgetful hearer but an active doer, this person will be blessed in what he does.
>
> James 1:19-25

The key for Jesus was to keep front of mind that we are to seek and pursue the righteousness of God (being in right relationship) and abide in the perfect law of liberty. We are to put into practice both of these values. We are to be a people of discovery above conclusions. Bob Rognlien[10] offers us some practical tools to be an effective doer of these values.

1. **Humility.** Start by reminding yourself you don't actually know it all.
2. **Read.** Take time to find credible sources that will give you new and reliable information.
3. **Listen.** Be willing to carefully consider perspectives different to your own.
4. **Learn.** Consider how those who differ from you can teach you new insights.
5. **Respect.** Demonstrate that you value those with different opinions.
6. **Love.** Openly express your love for people regardless of whether you agree or not.
7. **Submit.** Ask God what He is saying to you and what He wants you to do in faith.

---

10 Rognlien. B., (2020), The Adventure of a Jesus Shaped Life, *A House Divided: Standing Together in Polarized Times*, Retrieved from https://www.bobrognlien.com/blog/a-house-divided-standing-together-in-polarized-times on September 6th 2021

CHAPTER 2

APPLICATION TO DISCIPLESHIP

So, how do all of these thoughts find appropriate application in the context of discipleship? I am certainly not advocating that we can only express *perichoresis*, righteousness and a covenantal attitude with an open-ended, "You are accepted as you are", with no desire to encourage people towards becoming more like Jesus. A delight in spiritual formation assumes that followers of Jesus are pursuing becoming more like Him each and every day. Given this is the case, it becomes a matter of understanding the fuel driving the motivation to grow in Christ.

Paul helps us here by asserting that following the rules, living by prescribed standards, and pursuing social conformity is not the answer.

> *...because by the works of the Law none of mankind will be justified in His sight; for through the Law* **comes** *knowledge of sin.*
>
> Romans 3:20

These behaviours lead to a performance-based approach to living. This approach results in continuous appraisals of what is right and wrong. It establishes expectations that qualify people as being in and out. This all results in an environment where contractual relationships are the norm for living with God and one another. It becomes the seedbed for judgements and accusations, which is the work of the devil.

The fuel for empowered discipleship is:

— the work of the Holy Spirit in our lives;

> *And He, when He comes, will convict the world regarding sin, and righteousness, and judgment: regarding sin, because they do not believe in Me; and regarding righteousness, because I am going to the Father and you no longer* **are going to** *see Me; and regarding judgment, because the ruler of this world has been judged.*
>
> John 16:8-11

— the preaching and modelling of God's word;

> *I do not write these things to shame you, but to admonish you as my beloved children. For if you were to have countless tutors in Christ, yet* **you would** *not* **have** *many fathers, for in Christ Jesus I became your father through the gospel. Therefore I urge you, be imitators of me.*

1 Corinthians 4:14-16

— and sharing life together with others in close and accountable relationships.

Day by day continuing with one mind in the temple, and breaking bread from house to house, they were taking their meals together with gladness and sincerity of heart.

Acts 2:46

Greg Boyd's reflections on communities in the early church are helpful as we explore the idea of sharing the divine essence by how we live in oneness with one another.

> The members of the body of Christ are to minister *to one another.* The New Testament teaches that members of the body of Christ are to encourage one another (1 Thess.4:18; 5:11, 14; Heb. 10:24-25), confess sins to one another and pray for one another (James 5:16), speak the truth to one another (Eph.4:15, 25), care for one another (1 Cor.12:25; 1 Peter 4:10), admonish one another (Gal.6:1; Heb.3:13), and even confront one another. Indeed, we are to be willing to remove a member of our community from fellowship if he or she obstinately persists in sin that destroys him or her and/or threatens the community (Matt.18:15-18). We are, in short, called to lovingly help each other manifest our true identity in Jesus Christ. We are to help each other put off the old self and put on the new (Eph. 4:22-25).
>
> How can this be done without judgement? How can we possibly speak truth to others and hold them accountable if we aren't supposed to be looking for dust particles in others' lives? How can we possibly end fellowship with someone if we aren't supposed to judge others?
>
> If the New Testament's teaching on confession and accountability seems to us to stand in tension with its strong teaching against judgement, it is only because the New Testament presupposes an understanding of community that is largely absent in the modern church. Without this understanding of community, we don't have a context to obey in a healthy way the New Testament's teaching on the role of community in transforming us by holding us account-

able. When we try to apply this teaching outside the context of community as understood by the early church, it becomes judgement.

We know from a variety of sources, biblical and otherwise, that the early Christians met frequently - often daily - in each other's houses (Acts 2:46; Roms.16:5; 1 Cor. 16:19; Col.4:15; Philem.2; 2 John 10; cf Acts 8:3;12:12). They ate together, worshipped together, studied together, shared resources with one another, and lived life together in small clusters of house churches. Moreover, they frequently gathered in a hostile environment where the outside world could break in at any moment and take away their jobs, their houses, and even their lives. In other words, early Christians lived life in strongly bonded, intimate relationships with one another.

First century Christians also met in large, city-wide gatherings, to whatever degree their circumstances would allow them (Acts 1:13-15; 2:46; 5:12). But the *primary* gatherings (*ecclesia*, "church") in the early period were in people's homes. It wasn't until the fourth century that special religious buildings were devoted to Christians gathering in large groups.

Hence, when Paul or any other New Testament author wrote to "the church at" a certain locale, he was actually writing to various house churches in that region. The letter would be circulated to the various intimate gatherings in that area and eventually to house churches in other regions as well. So far as we can tell, these house churches would ordinarily consist of no more than forty or fifty people. Indeed, the church *as a whole* in any given region wouldn't have been very large when the New Testament was written. Paul's letters reveal that the church largely consisted of people who knew each other personally (e.g. Rom.16:3-23; 1 Cor.16:10-20; Col.4:10-15; 2 Tim.4:19-21).

The New Testament's teaching about our need to confess sin to one another and to hold each other accountable has to be understood against this background. In fact, the teaching can only be applied in a healthy, loving way in contexts such as a house church. Within contexts such as this, confession and accountability are simply what speaking the truth in love to one another looks like (Eph.4:15,25)

In a small group context, confession is healing, for it is done in trust, without the need to hide or perform. Within this context, accountability is beneficial, for it is carried out in the wisdom of love, which has taken the time to get on the inside of another's story. Feedback is offered not on the basis of abstract, idealistic principles of right and wrong, for the relationship is not conditioned by the knowledge of good and evil. Feedback is rather offered with a personal understanding and empathetic appreciation for the complex uniqueness of the person's concrete situation. For this reason, it is loving and helpful, not judgemental.

Loving and helpful confession and accountability are founded on a Spirit-created trust that grows out of life shared together. It cannot be demanded on the basis of a program or a rule. In intimate contexts, people are freed to be open about their struggles and to ask for help, for they fear no judgement. Nothing is forced; nothing is done with a motive to judge or shame. Each person grows in his or her walk with God with the loving assistance of the other members of the group. This is how the life of a disciple was meant to be lived.[11]

DESIGN AND DEFAULT

The foundation for this lifestyle of being in a trust-based community is simple yet profound and complex.

> *Therefore be imitators of God, as beloved children, and walk in love, just as Christ also loved you and gave Himself up for us, an offering and a sacrifice to God as a fragrant aroma.*
>
> Ephesians 5:1-2

It is apparently simple in that all we need to do is centre our spirituality around the New Testament commandment, "A new commandment I give to you, love one another as I have loved you, that you also love one another" (John 13:34)[12].

---

11 Boyd. G., Op. Cit. pg 217-219
12 Centering our spirituality around love and experiencing the love of God are thoughts I cover extensively in Radically Restored to Oneness with God. However, here is a brief summary.
Matthew 28:19-20 is the call to make disciples:

> Go therefore and make disciples of all nations, baptizing them in the name of the Father and the Son and the Holy Spirit, teaching them to observe all that I commanded you; and lo, I am with you always, even to the end of the age.

The phrase: 'teaching them to observe all I commanded you" is to be conducted in this way. All teaching, whether it is about worship, prayer, forgiveness, community etc., needs to be sourced and founded in observing all Jesus commanded. The word "observe" here means: 'to guard from loss by keeping your eyes upon'. Consequently, we re to make 'all I commanded you' the centre of our spirituality. Jesus gave us a new commandment that He owned as His for New Testament living.

> A new commandment I give to you, that you love one another, even as I have loved you, that you

CHAPTER 2

It is simultaneously profound as it assumes an experience of Jesus' love for us that is far more motivating and compelling than what we know intellectually: "and to know the love of Christ which surpasses knowledge, that you may be filled up to all the fullness of God." (Ephesians 3:19)

And it is also complex, as we have learnt to imitate the culture of the world we have been raised in, which has been strongly built on the foundation of another kingdom.

> *And you were dead in your offences and sins, in which you previously walked according to the course of this world, according to the prince of the power of the air, of the spirit that is now working in the sons of disobedience. Among them we too all previously lived in the lusts of our flesh, indulging the desires of the flesh and of the mind, and were by nature children of wrath, just as the rest.*
>
> Ephesians 2:1-3

This complexity requires an acknowledgement that in our pursuit of imitating God, we have positioned ourselves in a state of war. A state that if we don't engage with a designed strategy, we will lose by defaulting back to familiar ways and our own understanding.

> *But I say, walk by the Spirit, and you will not carry out the desire of the flesh. For the desire of the flesh is against the Spirit, and the Spirit*

---

also love one another. By this all men will know that you are My disciples, if you have love for one another. —John 13:34 – 35

This is My commandment, that you love one another, just as I have loved you... This I command you, that you love one another. —John 15:12 & 17

So, in making disciples, all our teaching needs to be sourced, through keeping front and centre the commandment Jesus gave us. This is reinforced in John 15:9-11:

Just as the Father has loved Me, I have also loved you; abide in My love. If you keep My commandments, you will abide in My love; just as I have kept My Father's commandments and abide in His love. These things I have spoken to you so that My joy may be in you, and that your joy may be full.

The love Jesus and the Father have for us are to be known by experience and encounter.

... and to know the love of Christ which surpasses knowledge, that you may be filled up to all the fullness of God.—Ephesians 3:19

The word 'to know' here means to know by experience and encounter. It is the same work in John 17:3 to know eternal life and in John 8:32 to know truth that sets you free. Experience and encounter creates heart knowledge which surpasses head knowledge. When love is the centre of spirituality it is a love from Jesus and Father we have experienced. This is why in Jesus' High Priestly prayer He prays:

I in them and You in Me, that they may be perfected in unity, so that the world may know that You sent Me, and loved them, even as You have loved Me. Father, I desire that they also, whom You have given Me, be with Me where I am, so that they may see My glory which You have given Me, for you loved Me before the foundation of the world. —John 17:23-24.

> *against the flesh; for these are in opposition to one another, in order to keep you from doing whatever you want. But if you are led by the Spirit, you are not under the Law.*

> Galatians 5:16-18

> *that the creation itself also will be set free from its slavery to corruption into the freedom of the glory of the children of God. For we know that the whole creation groans and suffers the pains of childbirth together until now. And not only **that**, but also we ourselves, having the first fruits of the Spirit, even we ourselves groan within ourselves, waiting eagerly for **our** adoption as sons **and daughters**, the redemption of our body.*

> Romans 8:21-23

As followers of Jesus, we are called to a lifestyle of spiritual formation.

> *For those whom He foreknew, He also predestined to become conformed to the image of His Son, so that He would be the firstborn among many brothers **and sisters;***

> Romans 8:29

> *And do not be conformed to this world, but be transformed by the renewing of your mind, so that you may prove what the will of God is, that which is good and acceptable and perfect.*

> Romans 12:2

> *But we all, with unveiled faces, looking as in a mirror at the glory of the Lord, are being transformed into the same image from glory to glory, just as from the Lord, the Spirit.*

> 2 Corinthians 3:18

> *So then, my beloved, just as you have always obeyed, not as in my presence only, but now much more in my absence, work out your own salvation with fear and trembling; for it is God who is at work in you, both to desire and to work for **His** good pleasure.*

> Philippians 2:12-13

A key element in our formation journey is designing an approach to the war between our flesh and our spirit. How do we build a life that lives in the spirit of life in Christ Jesus and acknowledges that we have been set free from the law of sin and of death (Romans 8:2)?

What do we need to do with an attitude of being willing to learn, discover and live with thoughtful application to live and walk by the Spirit?

> *But the fruit of the Spirit is love, joy, peace, patience, kindness, goodness, faithfulness, gentleness, and self-control; against such things there is no law. Now those who belong to Christ Jesus crucified the flesh with its passions and desires.*
>
> Galatians 5:22-24
>
> *For the mind set on the flesh is death, but the mind set on the Spirit is life and peace, because the mind set on the flesh is hostile toward God; for it does not subject itself to the law of God, for it is not even able* **to do so,** *and those who are in the flesh cannot please God.*
>
> Romans 8:6-8

What do we need to curtail in challenging circumstances, what is familiar, known and unconscious so that our mind is not set on the flesh?

> *Now the deeds of the flesh are evident, which are: sexual immorality, impurity, indecent behaviour, idolatry, witchcraft, hostilities, strife, jealousy, outbursts of anger, selfish ambition, dissensions, factions, envy, drunkenness, carousing, and things like these, of which I forewarn you, just as I have forewarned you, that those who practice such things will not inherit the kingdom of God.*
>
> Galatians 5:19-21

For mercy to triumph over judgement; for strife to not destroy the fabric of Kingdom community; to be an answer to Jesus' prayer that we would be one with one another, sharing the divine essence requires that we practise being 'sons of God':

> *So then, brothers **and sisters,** we are under obligation, not to the flesh, to live according to the flesh - for if you are living in accord with the flesh, you are going to die; but if by the Spirit you are putting to death the deeds of the body, you will live. For all who are being led by the Spirit of God, these are sons **and daughters** of God. For you have not received a spirit of slavery leading to fear again, but you have*

*received a spirit of adoption as sons **and daughters** by which we cry out, "Abba! Father!" The Spirit Himself testifies with our spirit that we are children of God, and if children, heirs also, heirs of God and fellow heirs with Christ, if indeed we suffer with **Him** so that we may also be glorified with **Him**.*

Romans 8:12-17

This is the subject of the next chapter.

SUMMARY

— *Perichoresis* highlights the fact that the Trinity live in community.

— As we are made in their image, we are called to live in community in the same way they do.

— Living in community, based in sharing the divine essence, requires a complete understanding of righteousness which includes right relationship with God, ourselves and others.

— Whatever builds up and promotes oneness with one another is righteous. Whatever breaks down and degrades relationships of oneness is unrighteous.

— Righteousness is a comprehensively relational reality.

— The Kingdom of God relies on covenant relationships as expressed by *perichoresis* and maintained by righteousness.

— Contractual relationships are transactional in nature based on expectations being met. They leave open the option of criticism or judgement being validated when expectations are not met.

— The way of love recognises justice as the restoration of peace in relationships, not the pain of punishment.

— New Testament communities were endeavouring to shape themselves on their experience of God's restorative justice in Jesus.

— Division and disunity are the inevitable fruit of a contractual attitude to relationships.

— We are to be people of discovery above conclusion.

- The complexity associated with imitating Jesus requires acknowledgement that we live in a state of war.

- A key element in our formation journey is designing an approach to the war between our flesh and our spirit.

QUESTIONS AND ACTIVITIES

A reminder, before you dive into considering each of these questions, take a moment to sit with Holy Spirit and ask Him to lead you and guide you. Ask Him to show you and highlight spaces where he wants to counsel you into freedom in this area.

1. How has your idea of community been impacted by the idea of *perichoresis*?

2. Can you identify three ways you promote oneness with others and three ways you degrade oneness with others?

3. What would need to change in you to move away from living contractually with others?

4. How could you offer 'restorative justice' to others when tension and conflict emerge in relationships?

5. How can you design an approach to the war between your flesh and your spirit? What would you focus on?

Chapter 3

A Call to Practice with Diligence

... Activity that Creates Oneness with Others

— What we practice determines who we become. A commitment to practice is a decision to live by design not by default

— To be diligent in practice is to posture and orientate our lives towards the work of the Word and the Spirit

— What does it look like to posture and orientate ourselves to diligently practice the characteristics of living in oneness with one another

— The life of God's Kingdom that is revealed through our oneness with one another makes it a target for demonic opposition and attack

— Knowing what the demonic will attack and how to resist.

I love reading a good biography. Having read many of them, I've observed a recurring theme reading about those who are stand-outs in their chosen field. They understand the power of practice. Psychology has found a direct statistical relationship between hours of practice and achievement. Practice isn't something you do once you become good at a skill. It's something you do that makes you good. Wolfgang Amadeus Mozart is a perfect example.

Mozart is known to have created compositions after long and laborious effort. He didn't just sit down and have instant proficiency in either playing the piano or composing music. Mozart trained, worked and struggled to develop his creative skills. He is reported to have practised for 8 to 10 hours a day from the age of 3. He was a practitioner of intense and diligent effort. Mozart, the most remarkable musical prodigy of all time, was successful because he practised with diligence.

A commitment to practice is a decision to live by design. It means that we prioritise certain activities in the way we live to ensure a particular outcome. It is the opposite to living by default, where outcomes are simply dreamed about without any consistent or deliberate activity that will bring them to pass.

With this in mind, it is no surprise that the Word of God directs us to consider what and how we practice.

> *By this the children of God and the children of the devil are obvious: anyone who does not **practice** righteousness is not of God, nor the one who does not love his brother and sister.*
>
> 1 John 3:10 (emphasis added)
>
> *Therefore I, the prisoner of the Lord, urge you to walk in a manner worthy of the calling with which you have been called, with all humility and gentleness, with patience, bearing with one another in love, being **diligent** to keep the unity of the Spirit in the bond of peace.*
>
> Eph. 4:1-3 (emphasis added)
>
> *But prove yourselves **doers** of the word, and not just hearers who deceive themselves. For if anyone is a hearer of the word and not a doer, he is like a man who looks at his natural face in a mirror; for once he has looked at himself and gone away, he has immediately forgotten what kind of person he was.*
>
> James 1:22-24 (emphasis added)

CHAPTER 3

PRACTICE AND INHERITANCE

What we practice affects what we inherit: "those who practice such things will NOT inherit the Kingdom of God" (Gal. 5:21). Then after a long list of characteristics we are to practice in Ephesians, Paul writes:

> *For this you know with certainty, that no sexually immoral or impure or greedy person, which amounts to an idolater, has an inheritance in the kingdom of Christ and God.*
>
> Ephesians 5:5

These Scriptures would indicate that while we can be in the Kingdom of God, born again and adopted into the family of God, we can experience different levels of inheritance. This proposition appears to be supported by Paul when he writes:

> *According to the grace of God which was given to me, like a wise master builder I laid a foundation, and another is building on it. But each person must be careful how he builds on it. For no one can lay a foundation other than the one which is laid, which is Jesus Christ. Now if anyone builds on the foundation with gold, silver, precious stones, wood, hay, or straw, each one's work will become evident; for the day will show it because it is to be revealed with fire, and the fire itself will test the quality of each one's work. If anyone's work which he has built on it remains, he will receive a reward. If anyone's work is burned up, he will suffer loss; but he himself will be saved, yet only so as through fire.*
>
> 1 Cor. 3:10-15

Paul is clear that while we are saved, what we build our lives with, will result in reward and loss. Wood, hay and straw are familiar elements, somewhat easy to access in an agricultural community. On the other hand, gold, silver, and precious stones require being searched out and discovered.

We choose whether we build with wood, hay and straw – the familiar elements of our surrounding culture, or to build with gold, silver and precious stones. As followers of Jesus, regardless of how we build, Jesus will be with us. That is His promise. However, for those that choose to build with wood, hay and straw, the pursuit of Jesus' life, grace, and mercy are not a priority. These builders generally live by default, being shaped and formed by the surrounding culture. They neglect to discover, search out and practice the ways of Kingdom culture when responding to their circumstances and in their relationships. In contrast, those who choose to build with gold, silver and precious stones live a lifestyle of practice, of consistently dreaming and pursuing, searching out and discovering how they can expand their comprehension and expression of what they have given themselves to. They intentionally pursue Kingdom culture through their daily practices.

Jesus' teaching around stewardship carries echoes of reward and loss when the master returns.

> *"For it is just like a man about to go on a journey, who called his own slaves and entrusted his possessions to them. To one he gave five talents, to another, two, and to another, one, each according to his own ability; and he went on his journey. The one who had received the five talents immediately went and did business with them and earned five more talents. In the same way the one who had received the two talents earned two more. But he who received the one talent went away and dug a hole in the ground, and hid his master's money.*
>
> *"Now after a long time the master of those slaves came and settled accounts with them. The one who had received the five talents came up and brought five more talents, saying, 'Master, you entrusted five talents to me. See, I have earned five more talents.' His master said to him, 'Well done, good and faithful slave. You were faithful with a few things, I will put you in charge of many things; enter the joy of your master.'*
>
> *"Also the one who had received the two talents came up and said, 'Master, you entrusted two talents to me. See, I have earned two more talents.' His master said to him, 'Well done, good and faithful slave. You were faithful with a few things, I will put you in charge of many things; enter the joy of your master.'*
>
> *"Now the one who had received the one talent also came up and said, 'Master, I knew you to be a hard man, reaping where you did not sow, and gathering where you did not scatter seed. And I was afraid, so I went away and hid your talent in the ground. See, you still have what is yours.'*
>
> *"But his master answered and said to him, 'You worthless, lazy slave! Did you know that I reap where I did not sow, and gather where I did not scatter seed? Then you ought to have put my money in the*

> bank, and on my arrival I would have received my money back with interest. Therefore: take the talent away from him, and give it to the one who has the ten talents.'
>
> "For to everyone who has, more shall be given, and he will have an abundance; but from the one who does not have, even what he does have shall be taken away. And throw the worthless slave into the outer darkness; in that place there will be weeping and gnashing of teeth.
>
> Matt.25:14-30

How the servants traded with what they had received determined what reward or loss, they experienced. The Kingdom of God is "righteousness, peace and joy in the Holy Spirit" (Romans 14:17). These are all gifts we have received from Jesus. It seems clear that how we 'trade' with what we have received and build with what we have discovered impacts our inheritance after death. What we do and practise here on earth has an eternal consequence: practice and diligence have their outcomes.

PRACTICE AND DILIGENCE

Practice and diligence begin with our inner consent to surrender to the ways of God and the values of His Kingdom.

> Now He was questioned by the Pharisees as to when the kingdom of God was coming, and He answered them and said, "The kingdom of God is not coming with signs that can be observed; nor will they say, 'Look, here it is! or, 'There **it is!**' For behold, the Kingdom of God is in your midst (is within you).
>
> Luke 17:20-21

Jesus states that the Kingdom of God is not an external circumstance; instead, it is an inner reality when we have consented to God's view of reality. It results from our response to God's invitation to participate in His unfolding story with mankind. Our participation bears fruit which is an expression of the Kingdom, not the Kingdom itself.

Central to God's view of reality is our radical restoration to oneness with Him: "that they may also be in us" (John 17:21). As we are now one with God, we are to live in oneness with one another: "that they may all be one" (John 17:21). As I have previously noted, when Paul writes, "Therefore, I the prisoner of the Lord, implore you to walk in a manner worthy of your calling with which you have been called" (Ephesians 4:1), the application of 'calling' is to live from our oneness with God (Ephesians 1:1-2:10) in pursuing oneness with one another (Ephesians 2:11-3:21). Paul not only implores us to pursue oneness but also reinforces his call by emphasising the need for diligence: "Being *diligent* to preserve the unity of the Spirit in the bond of peace" (Ephesians 4:3 – emphasis added).

Understanding that we are to be diligent raises the questions: How are we to be diligent? What are we to be diligent in? Put simply; it is to be led by the Spirit in expressing love and devotion to one another. Being led by the Spirit because Christ is within us (Colossians 1:27) is absolutely paramount.

> *If Christ is in you, though the body is dead because of sin, yet the spirit is alive because of righteousness. For all who are being led by the Spirit of God, these are sons and daughters of God. For you have not received a spirit of slavery leading to fear again, but you have received a spirit of adoption as sons and daughters by which we cry out, "Abba! Father!" The Spirit Himself testifies with our spirit that we are children of God, and if children, heirs also, heirs of God and fellow heirs with Christ, if indeed we suffer with Him so that we may also be glorified with Him.*
>
> Rom. 8:10, 14-17

The New Testament has very helpful lists of what it looks like to pursue living in oneness with one another. However, before we look at these, it is essential to note that a life of following Jesus is not to be joined to self-effort. Although diligence, perseverance and discipline are required, these characteristics are to orientate and posture us towards the life and work of the Spirit. They are not to empower our own efforts to behave according to the 'lists'. This is seen clearly in Romans 12:11, wherein the midst of one of the most extensive lists, Paul writes:

> *not lagging behind in diligence, fervent in spirit, serving the Lord; rejoicing in hope, persevering in tribulation, devoted to prayer,*

It is the Holy Spirit who calls us into our righteousness and moves to silence the shame, guilt and condemnation of the devil.[1] The Spirit is our helper, counsellor and comforter who reminds us of the empowering presence of grace available to us to become a more complete disciple of Jesus.

---

1 These truths are extensively explored in *Radically Restored to Oneness with God.*

CHAPTER 3

Pressure and challenging circumstances reveal what's inside of us. If you squeeze a lemon, you get lemon juice. If you squeeze an orange, you get orange juice. When negative circumstances and relational pressure squeeze a Christian, you should get 'Jesus juice'. Jesus juice is made up of the fruit of the Spirit. This fruit is born as a result of living from and being empowered by the root source of the fruit: the Spirit. It is not called the fruit of 'ticking off the list of behaviours' that describe what oneness with one another looks like!

When Jesus juice doesn't come out when we are under pressure, an area for the work of grace is identified. Through self-awareness and personal responsibility, we can invite the work of the Spirit and grace into that area to help us be transformed into the image of Jesus. This is our destiny.[2]

> *By this, love is perfected with us, so that we may have confidence in the day of judgment; because as He is, we also are in this world.*
>
> 1 John 4:17

Reading John 17:20-21, we discover that Jesus believed that a primary way we should be in the world is living in pursuit of oneness with one another.

> *I am not asking on behalf of these alone, but also for those who believe in Me through their word, that they may all be one; just as You, Father, are in Me and I in You, that they also may be in Us, so that the world may believe that You sent me.*

In His prayer, Jesus highlights four practices that, when practised diligently and empowered by the Spirit, will accelerate our pursuit of living in oneness with one another.

First, "the glory which You have given to Me, I have given to them, that they may be one, just as We are one" (John 17:22). Here, the word 'glory' means: "to offer a personal opinion that gives value". Jesus states that the Father makes declarations about Jesus that honour and bestow value on Him. Jesus, in turn, does the same to you and me. His declarations over us are designed to underline who we are in Him. They also set the standard by which we are to relate to and treat one another. Jesus' oneness with God is empowered by opinions that give value. Jesus' oneness with us is empowered in the same way. Therefore, we will empower our oneness with one another by practising ONLY offering opinions of others that give them value! What a life-changing practice this would be for God's people!

---

2   These ideas are fully explored in *Radically Restored to Oneness with God* and will be addressed again in the next chapter.

Second, "I in them and You in Me, that they may be perfected in unity" (John 17:23). We are empowered in our pursuit of oneness with one another when we understand that becoming one is a process; it is something that is *being* perfected. We grow in revelation knowledge of the mystery that Christ dwells in us; as we rely on this truth, we grow into our predestined conformity to Jesus.

Third, "and loved them even as You have loved Me" (John 17:23). When we increasingly know, that we know, that we know, in our heart, that the Father loves us just the same as He loves Jesus, we are empowered for oneness with one another. We are to love one another as Jesus loves us. The key to our love for one another is the depth of heart knowledge we carry of God's love for us. Jesus is praying for you to have encounters with His love (Ephesians 3:19). He wants to empower your desire to live in oneness with others. We are to practice seeking experience and encounters with His love.

Fourth, "I have made Your *name* known to them, and will make it known, so that the love with which You loved Me may be in them, and I in them" (John 17:26 – emphasis added). Here we need to remind ourselves that this prayer from Jesus is for us: "I do not ask on behalf of these alone, but for THOSE ALSO who believe in Me through their word" (John 17:20). One of the best ways to get to know God is to know His names. There are over 100 in the Bible. When we know God's character and his nature and how that translates to his actions and ways, we are empowered to be with one another in the same ways. We are to practice knowing the names of God.

WHAT TO PRACTICE

As a child, I was taught to cross the road as part of the process of getting from one place to another. I was taught to STOP, LOOK AND LISTEN. The lists that follow are extraordinarily important. Whether you choose to diligently posture and orientate yourself towards these behaviours or not will impact and affect your inheritance. As you read, can I encourage you to 'STOP, LOOK and LISTEN'? STOP and ask Holy Spirit to lead you and guide you. LOOK with Holy Spirit for the areas where He is inviting you into upgrade, for transformation through grace. Often these will be areas you struggle with or fail in. Then LISTEN to what He says & shows you that will enable you to grow and become an answer to Jesus' prayer. Then act – cross the road with your hand in His to go from where you are now to where He is calling you. Put into diligent practise those things that He shows you.

1 Timothy 4:7-8 provides instructive wisdom here:

But have nothing to do with worldly fables fit only for old women. On the other hand, discipline yourself for the purpose of godliness; for bodily discipline is only of little profit, but godliness is profitable for all things, since it holds promise for the present life and also for the life to come.

Everyone who is training has markers. Markers are important for accountability and progress.

Romans 12:9-21 describes what oneness with one another looks like when it states:

— Let love be without hypocrisy

— Abhor what is evil; cling to what is good

— Be devoted to one another in brotherly love

— Outdo one another in showing honour

— Contribute to the needs of the saints

— Practice hospitality

— Bless those who persecute you. Bless and do not curse

— Rejoice with those who rejoice

— Weep with those who weep

— Do not be haughty in mind

— Associate with the lowly

— Do not be wise in your own estimation

— Never pay back evil for evil to anyone

— Respect what is right in the eyes of all men

— Be at peace with all men where possible as it depends on you

— Overcome evil with good.

SELAH

1 Corinthians 13:4-8 shows us the most excellent way to live as a follower of Jesus. Don't forget to STOP. LOOK. LISTEN.

- Love is patient under stress
- Love is kind at all times
- Love is generous, not envious
- Love is humble, not self-promoting
- Love is never rude
- Love does not manipulate by using shame
- Love is not irritable or easily offended
- Love celebrates honesty
- Love does not focus on what is flawed
- Love is loyal to the end

SELAH

As we put on the new self, which has been created in righteousness and holiness of the truth in the likeness of God, we need to STOP. LOOK. LISTEN AGAIN. (Ephesians 4:24-5:5).

- Lay aside falsehood; speak the truth
- Do not allow anger to cause you to sin
- Do not give the devil an opportunity
- Do not steal
- Labour to be generous
- Speak what gives grace to those who hear
- Don't grieve the Holy Spirit
- Let all bitterness, wrath, anger, clamour, slander and malice be put away from you
- Be kind, tender-hearted and forgiving towards each other
- Walk in love
- Put aside immorality, impurity and greed
- Give thanks, not filthiness, silly talk or coarse jesting.

CHAPTER 3

SELAH

While there are other lists, my last from Colossians 3:5-17 will serve you well if you STOP. LOOK. LISTEN.

- Be dead to immorality, impurity, passion, evil desires, greed
- Put aside anger, wrath, malice, slander, and abusive speech
- Do not lie to one another
- Put on a heart of compassion, kindness, humility, gentleness and patience
- Bear with one another
- Forgive one another of complaints
- Let the peace of Christ rule in your hearts
- Be thankful
- Let the word richly dwell within you
- With all wisdom, teach and admonish one another
- Sing with thankfulness in your hearts to God
- Do everything in the name of our Lord Jesus
- Give thanks through Jesus to God the Father.

When our lives embrace loving one another through these postures and orientations, we naturally step into what Paul describes:

> *Do nothing from selfishness or empty conceit, but with humility consider one another as more important than yourselves; do not merely look out for your own personal interests, but also for the interests of others.*
>
> Phil. 2:3-4

What a glorious life we have been invited into.

WEAPONS AND INSIGHTS

Commitment to being one with others, by definition, requires dedication and effort. Being one with others is easy when everything is going well, we agree and have no qualms with each other. However, our oneness with others will come under pressure here on earth, and we experience success and failure caused by fractures in our hearts. Culturally, there is low confidence in the genuineness of others which undermines our life with one another. There are so many internal and external landmines and hurdles to negotiate in our pursuit of relational wellness. Additionally, Kinnaman and Mattock observe that:

> "Most of the ways we measure and experience 'church' involve doing things FOR people, not necessarily being WITH people. We have to change the imbalance of program over presence. Doing so will help us create a healthier emotional climate together."[3]

We live in a time when followers of Jesus need to rediscover the practice of Spirit-filled faithfulness in a culture overrun with allegiance to self. The permission that people give themselves to place their opinions above serving others is growing exponentially. Add to this the social media culture that validates all opinions as equal; there is a coercive influence away from being members of each other.

It is my experience that commitment from the people of God to being one with others is rapidly breaking down. Divorce rates inside the church are equivalent to those outside the church. Business partners who are followers of Jesus participate in bitter and spiteful relational breakdowns over money. In the last few years, I have personally watched the destructive process associated with the use of power, criticism and judgement result in three capable church leaders being removed from office. Then there are my own personal experiences over 30 years of leading the church I founded of: betrayal by those I have empowered; personal criticism; lies and gossip because of theological differences; and a significant church split.

Through all of these experiences, I have seen patterns that provide insights into how to stand against the degradation of unity and fight for oneness with one another. In observation, meditation and considering my circumstances, I have noticed particular weapons that are designed to rob, steal and destroy the life of God. These weapons are aimed against three targets: our knowledge of God, how we see one another: and what we know about ourselves. If the enemy can weaken us in any one of these three areas, the strength of our oneness is compromised.

---

3   Kinnaman. D., & Matlock. M., (2019). *Faith for Exiles*, Bailer Books, pg 134.

CHAPTER 3

OUR KNOWLEDGE OF GOD

How we love one another reveals how much we know God.

> *Beloved, let us love one another; for love is from God, and everyone who loves has been born of God and knows God. The one who does not love does not know God, because God is love.*
>
> 1 John 4:7-8

We have already established from Ephesians 3:19 that we can know the love of Christ through experience and encounter. Or we can know the love of Christ intellectually. We have heart knowledge, and we have head knowledge. John is advocating that we can assess how much we know God in our hearts from the way that we love others. Scazzaro describes the disparity between head and heart knowledge like this: "we can boldly preach truths we don't live."[4]

John adds further to his insights when he writes:

> *If someone says, "I love God," and yet he hates his brother or sister, he is a liar; for the one who does not love his brother and sister whom he has seen, cannot love God, whom he has not seen.*
>
> 1 John 4:20

The Greek word for hate here means to disregard, disrespect, detest and dismiss as unimportant. When God's people act this way, they are not fulfilling the New Testament commandment to 'love one another as I have loved you.' And yet relational breakdown is often underpinned by disregard, disrespect, detesting and dismissing as unimportant. Unfortunately, God's people aren't immune from thinking this way and acting from these attitudes. This approach to relating with others is often highlighted when God's people begin to live for 'a cause'. The causes may include: doctrinal purity; proving betrayal; criticism of leadership styles and practice; treatment of others such as same-sex orientated people; unmet cultural expectations.

A cause-driven approach to relationships primarily draws its energy and life from what it is against. People with this approach judge and determine that 'their truth' needs to be adopted by others. The belief that there is the need to prosecute what they believe is right or wrong creates 'good guys' and 'bad guys'. Those who are 'in' and those who are 'out'. Their view of reality moves from being founded in love to being founded in the rightness of certain beliefs

---

[4] Scazzero. P., (2015). *The Emotionally Healthy Leader*. Zondervan, Michigan pg 117

and behaviours. As a result, they become dismissive of others' perspectives, disrespectful of their personhood, detesting how they live and disregarding the emotional impact they cause others to experience. In biblical language, they 'hate' others.

How can the weapons formed against us cause such responses from God's people? Primarily because their heart knowledge of God is not sufficient in moments of relational pressure and tension. However, it is in our pursuit of becoming one that we can look in the mirror and honestly appraise our lack of oneness with others.

Stanley offers the following insights that help us here:

> For whoever does not love their brother and sister whom they have seen, *cannot* love God, who they have not seen.

"Cannot love God"?

That's strong.

"Cannot" is a reference to opportunity, not ability. If I don't get on the bus, I cannot ride the bus. Not because I lack the ability to ride, but because I lost my opportunity by not getting on the bus, to begin with. To refuse to love a brother or sister is to forego the opportunity to love God.

John placed little value on feelings of love and appreciation for God. Understandably so. He watched Jesus bleed to death. He was not confused. Jesus didn't pay for sin via fond feelings and heartfelt compassion. John's sin cost Jesus his life. It was Jesus' sacrificial display of love that paved the way for John's sins to be erased. For John, *un*displayed love was no love at all. He says as much:

> This is how we know what love is: Jesus Christ laid down His life for us. And we ought to lay down our lives for our brothers and sisters…
> Dear children, let us not love with words or speech but with actions and truth.

For John, Paul and Jesus, loving people *is* loving God. Not because people are God, but because they are loved by God. Refusing to love a brother or sister actively is paramount to refusing to love God. Under the new covenant, we do not love God *and* love our neighbours. Under the new covenant, we love God *by* loving our neighbours. So, once more, with feeling:

> For whoever does not love their brother and sister, whom they have seen, cannot love God, whom they have not seen.

It's not the religious hoops we jump through, the prayers we pray, the sins we have confessed, or even the communion crackers we've consumed that demonstrate our love for the Father. It's far less complicated than that.

While preparing to share this content with our churches for the first time, I was struck by a thought that immediately brought tears to my eyes. Before including it in my message outline, I decided to run it by Sandra. With no context and no hint as to why I was asking, I walked into the kitchen and asked:

> Is there anything that brings you more satisfaction and joy in life than watching our children love each other?

Now, the correct answer would have been, "Next to spending time alone with you, Andy..." But I wasn't fishing for affirmation. I was genuinely curious. She paused for a moment and shook her head. "No," she said. "I can't think of anything that fills me up more than watching our kids talk, share, laugh together, and love each other.

I can't either.

I wonder where we get that?

If John is correct, we may well have gotten it from our Father in heaven. It may be a reflection of the image of God embedded on our souls.

> Did I mention that if you mistreat one of my kids, all the singing and offering-taking in the world won't make up for it? Did I mention that the best way to honour me is to honour my children?[5]

The impact of these thoughts on our oneness with others can be ascertained when we honestly ask ourselves: do I genuinely bless those who persecute me and not curse them, and am I really able to put away bitterness, wrath, anger, clamour, slander and malice?

---

5   Stanley. A., (2018). *Irresistible*, Zondervan, Michigan pg 229-231

The ability to love as Jesus loves, in the face of our or others' 'truth-based judgements' so that we don't disregard, disrespect or dismiss others, is empowered by a biblical understanding of justice. Gillard helps put into context how the pursuit of a cause can be wrapped in God's love instead of a need to be right.

> The more accurate description of biblical justice is restorative justice. Biblically, justice is a divine act of reparation where breached relationships are renewed and victims, offenders, and communities are restored. Justice, therefore, is about relationships and our conduct within them. Justice asks, How is righteousness embodied and exuded in how I live in relation to God, neighbour, and creation? In fact, Scripture could be read as the narrative of God's restorative justice unfolding in the world.
>
> Righteousness is *mishpat,* the justice of God, enacted. Jeremias says, "Righteousness is the outcome of a functioning justice." The concepts of righteousness and justice are intended to pattern the lives of God's people, governing the church's relational ethics. When righteousness and justice are wed, as they are about forty times in Scripture, the surest implication is social justice.
>
> The Hebrew and Greek words for justice and righteousness often occur together. In fact, the prophet Amos never speaks of righteousness without justice. Righteousness, therefore, cannot be experienced without justice. Justice is the foundation of righteousness. Justice and righteousness are the indispensable presuppositions for Israel's worship and existence (Amos 5,7,15,21-24). Theologian Jorge Jeremias writes that "justice and righteousness are the most precious gifts of God to his people.[6]

Here are some thoughts on what to diligently practise so that you take every opportunity to love others from your knowledge of God.

1. Posture your heart through worship, prayer, reading the Word, thankfulness and joy to seek and receive regular encounters with God's love.

2. Meditate on: 'that you sent Me, and loved them, EVEN AS YOU HAVE LOVED ME' (John 17:23) and 'so that the love with which you loved Me, MAY BE IN THEM, and I in them (John 17:26).

---

6 "Dubois Gillard. D., (2018). *Rethinking Incarceration,* IVP Books pg 138-142

3. Forgive others by asking them questions of discovery in order to understand their perspective. Avoid treating others based on your own untested conclusions.

4. Never assume you know and therefore judge the intent and motives behind another's actions. Ask them.

5. Find security and assurance in who you are in Christ. Rely on His opinions of you, beginning with being holy, chosen and beloved. Resist allowing the opinions of others to be taken personally so that you are neither spoiled by success nor shattered by failure.

6. Adopt the value of only ever offering personal opinions that give others value (John 17:22) and nothing else.

7. Abide in His love and follow the New Testament Commandment (John 13:34-35) by monitoring your self-talk to discover the non-Kingdom places you are dwelling in in your inner world. Then repent and ask for His empowering presence (grace) to guide you.

That's all well and good, but what about when others don't take up the opportunity to love you? When you are betrayed, lied about, accused, judged, criticised or neglected? Here are some ideas (tried and tested through my own experiences and those of people I walk with) of what to diligently practise in these moments!

1. Focus on the PRIZE of who you can become and who Jesus can be for you. Don't dwell on the PRICE you are paying for the unjust treatment you are receiving.

2. Find your hope in Jesus, not in the pain being experienced going away (Rom. 5:1-5). When inner turmoil (tribulation) is your experience, embrace the process of endurance, character development and renewed hope. It is here that you can find the love of God being poured out in your heart.

3. Embrace the inevitable experiences of suffering (Rom. 8:17) as a place of opportunity to escape the prisons of wrong belief and enter into your destiny to be conformed into His image. (Rom. 8:29)

HOW WE SEE ONE ANOTHER

The second target for weapons that are designed to rob, steal and destroy the life of God is: how we see one another.

How we see someone impacts how we treat them.

> *When the woman saw that the tree was good for food, and that it was a delight to the eyes, and that the tree was desirable to make one wise, she took some of its fruit and ate; and she also gave some to her husband with her, and he ate. Then the eyes of both of them were opened, and they knew that they were naked; and they sewed fig leaves together and made themselves waist coverings.*
>
> *Now they heard the sound of the Lord God walking in the garden in the cool of the day, and the man and his wife hid themselves from the presence of the Lord God among the trees of the garden.*
>
> Gen. 3:6-8

When Adam and Eve's picture of God changed, so did their attitude towards Him and, consequently, their behaviour: they hid themselves. Their initial picture and experience of God had been as a loving Father with whom they walked and co-laboured. Now, with a different picture, they became afraid of God.

I have watched this dynamic play out in marriages as one spouse refuses to speak to the person they were once infatuated with. I have seen it occur within church contexts where friends in positions of influence as Elders decide that the Senior Pastor, who is also their friend, is controlling and unsuitable to lead. After gathering an army of people to their side, they prosecute their case and the Senior Pastor is sacked, impacting not only the pastor but the entire community. Personally, I have experienced the pain of betrayal and being cast as the bad guy by people who I have counted as friends, who I have sown years, sometimes even decades into.

How can weapons formed against us cause these responses from God's people? The way I've seen it play out is that a moment of misunderstanding or pain of some sort occurs. This leads to perceptions of motive, intent and character of a person being created. These then begin to inform responses to a perceived reality of who and what they are and what they did that is believed to be true. Feelings are very real. However, that doesn't make them the best arbiter of what is true. Feelings are good messengers but terrible masters.

In all these situations, someone draws a circle and places some on the inside as being right and others on the outside who are wrong. What would happen if, whenever we face moments of misunderstanding or pain, we all chose to draw bigger circles around Jesus that include them all as one.

CHAPTER 3

Jesus prayed for us that we would be perfected and become like Him in the pursuit of unity. Therefore, when living in real oneness, love towards one another is more fully discovered and practised when there is disunity, disadvantage, relational pressure, tension, disagreement and difficult people. When we recognise the importance of oneness to God, we prize, value, and pursue it at all costs, in most circumstances. When there is abuse, whether spiritual, psychological, emotional or physical the restoration of relationship may no longer be desirable because it would be unsafe.

The guiding question for the spirituality of a follower of Jesus, in every relationship, whether it is good, bad or indifferent, is: What does love require of me?

To answer this question well, it is necessary to define what love is and what it is not accurately. Love is a decision of the heart to delight in another and to will their good ahead of your own. Love is redemptive in purpose, nature and outworking, believing there was original intent for relationships. Love is NOT: a feeling of happiness or desire for another person; nor is it an understanding that permits people to 'be themselves' and to 'do what is right in their own eyes'.

> *Now I ask you, lady, not as though I were writing to you a new commandment, but the one which we have had from the beginning, that we love one another.*
>
> 2 John 1:5

A life of following Jesus is not complicated, but it does require an attitude of discovery. When we are Spirit led, no matter the condition of a relationship, He will always encourage us towards kindness, goodness, gentleness, faithfulness and self-control (Gal.5:22-23). This results in the call to diligently practise a love that requires something from me and does not place a demand on others.

The greatest attribute we have received from the Father is our free will. The ten commandments have been proclaimed as God's demands for how we should live. However, in the context of free will they are an invitation to choose how to live in right relationship with God and one another. They establish the Fathers expectancy that we would adopt them from love expressed through our free will.

We are to do all we can to protect this approach to love.

> *This is His commandment, that we believe in the name of His Son Jesus Christ, and love one another, just as He commanded us. The one who keeps His commandments remains in Him, and He in him. We know by this that He remains in us, by the Spirit whom He has given us.*

1 John 3:23-24

Jesus gave us a new commandment, to love one another as He loved us. It is not a suggestion. It is not a proposition for our consideration. It is a clear and present expectancy of how we are to live. The word 'keep' in verse 23 means 'to protect'. The imagery here can be illustrated by the thought of a violent intruder set on killing us, arriving at my home when we are together as a family: grandparents, children with spouses, and grandchildren. As the "heroic patriarch", I yell the instruction to the men to protect the women and grandchildren by moving them to the bedrooms, doing everything we can to keep them safe. So, the word 'keep' here means we do everything in our power to protect what is valuable. We protect "loving one another as Jesus loved us".

We protect this love when: we honour others as God honoured us by giving His Son to die for our dishonouring sin; we offer others value and worth as God offered us by giving His only Son for my right standing with Him, and we endeavour to repair broken relationships as God gave us right relationship with Him through being adopted into His family.

We see others properly, do what love requires and act in ways that protect love when we are of one heart and mind with Paul:

> *Now may our God and Father Himself, and our Lord Jesus, direct our way to you; and may the Lord cause you to increase and overflow in love for one another, and for all people, just as we also do for you; so that He may establish your hearts blameless in holiness before our God and Father at the coming of our Lord Jesus with all His saints.*
>
> 1 Thess. 3:11-13

We are to pursue heart to heart relationships based in humility, transparency, vulnerability and being able to find a reverse gear. These things are not easy! Simple, but not easy. Because of this, we tend to move toward functional relationships focused on tasks, objectives and outcomes. When these are the basis of doing life together, unmet expectations lead to criticism and judgement emerging from the shadows of our best intentions.

When we are genuinely looking for oneness with one another, we don't have to see eye to eye on everything to walk hand in hand on some things. This is particularly relevant when the value of oneness with others is considered in the light of how the body of Christ is to live together. A unity that doesn't demand uniformity but celebrates diversity.

Historically the pursuit of being one has been expressed through ecumenical activity and events for the sake of cooperative effort. Invariably, this cooperative effort has been limited by: the vested interests of each group, each group pursuing their own agenda; transactional relationships; and looking for the lowest common denominator of approval. The net result is some level of unity of purpose for the sake of unity.

While we need to honour ecumenical activity and what has been achieved through historical efforts, we need to be courageous enough to follow the Spirit in reimagining how the pursuit of being one can be expressed. I see the beginnings of the people of God coming together in activity and events for the sake of investment in one another. An investment that desires long term relationships; is based on a willingness to be vulnerable, that discovers together the road to oneness, and that recognises the power of acceptance even when we disagree. All of this is because unity of heart is the way of the Kingdom for the sake of those outside the Kingdom being able to see the God who is love.

This is reconciled diversity which moves way beyond cooperative effort.

With all of this in mind, I am reminded that in the Australian outback, the large cattle herds are managed by digging wells for water rather than erecting fences to keep them contained. Why? Cattle need water and will stay close to its source.

For over 2000 years, God has dug many 'wells' of revival and reformation worldwide for people to drink from. Yet man wants to build 'fences' around what the well has provided and represents. The fences are constructed out of doctrinal beliefs and ecclesiastical practices. Man then assumes he is defending the honour of God by defending and repairing 'their' fenced area from others who have fenced off 'their' well.

As we honour the wells God has dug and stop building, defending and repairing the fences, we will find reconciled diversity; the pursuit of oneness; being the answer to Jesus' prayer; the honouring of Paul's view of the church, and see the tremendous spiritual impact on those yet to believe in Jesus.

The impact of these thoughts on our oneness with others can be ascertained when we honestly ask ourselves: do I share honour, or do I focus on what is flawed in others?

Honour is the operating system of the Kingdom of God. The Trinity relate to one another in honour.

But when He, the Spirit of truth, comes, He will guide you into all the truth; for He will not speak on His own, but whatever He hears, He will speak; and He will disclose to you what is to come. He will glorify Me, for He will take from Mine and will disclose it to you. All things that the Father has are Mine; this is why I said that He takes from Mine and will disclose it to you.

John 16:13-15

Jesus spoke these things; and raising His eyes to heaven, He said, "Father, the hour has come; glorify Your Son, so that the Son may glorify You, just as You gave Him authority over all mankind, so that to all whom You have given Him, He may give eternal life.

John 17:1-2

Then God said, "Let Us make mankind in Our image, according to Our likeness; and let them rule over the fish of the sea and over the birds of the sky and over the livestock and over all the earth, and over every crawling thing that crawls on the earth."

Gen.1:26

The Trinity honours those they have made and who serve them:

*Yet You have made him a little lower than God,
And You crown him with glory and majesty!
You have him rule over the works of Your hands;
You have put everything under his feet,*

Psalm 8:5-6

The one who loves his life loses it, and the one who hates his life in this world will keep it to eternal life. If anyone serves Me, he must follow Me; and where I am, there My servant will be also; if anyone serves Me, the Father will honour him.

John 12:25-26

This operating system is exemplified throughout scripture:

— Honour your father and mother (Ex. 20:12)

— Husbands honour your wife (1 Pet. 3:7)

- Slaves honour your master (1 Tim. 6:1)

- Honour governing authorities and their office, regardless of character (Rom. 13:1-4)

- Honour spiritual leaders (1 Tim. 5:17)

- Honour those who are weaker (1 Cor. 12:23-24)

- Honour God with our body (1 Cor. 6:12-20)

- Honour one another (Rom. 12:10)

The operating system of western cultures has rushed towards contempt in the last fifteen years. In particular, a culture of dishonour has gained ascendancy in social media and politics. It is expressed through sarcasm, personal insults, increasing entitlement, scorn, arrogance, disgust, anger, cynicism and the 'cancel culture.'

Honour ascribes value to others. It recognises the IMAGO DEI in everyone. Honour is expressed through humility, respect, gratitude, appreciation and acknowledgement. It is others centred and offers life to all. Dishonour lowers the value of others. It brings resentment towards those with higher cultural status, anger towards those with equal cultural status, and contempt towards those with lower cultural status. Dishonour focuses on an aspect of another person's life and makes it the whole or majority of who they are. It thrives on the echo chamber of friends both online and in person.

Honour creates a safe place of trust when there is conflict. Dishonour activates deep fear and sabotages attempts at reconciliation.

Honour creates access to blessing and the spiritual authority another carries. Dishonour closes access to blessing and cuts us off from what another has to offer.

Honour brings out the best in people. Dishonour brings out the worst in people.

Honour results in a kind and loyal care for the well-being of another. The Hebrew word for this is *Hesed*. The Greek word for this is *Agape*. Where *Hesed* and *Agape* are central to oneness with one another, then people are bound together by strong and lasting attachments. Wilder and Hendricks offer the following fascinating insights about attachment:

> Attachment is the strongest force in the human brain. It is not an emotion, although we feel strongly, and attachment runs much deeper in

the brain below wilful control. Attachment is the best word scientists could find for what glues people together and little creatures to their parents. It produces an enduring care for the well-being of another. Attachment is a life-giving forever bond with no mechanism in the brain to unglue us. If God has an enduring love for us that brings us good, the only force in the human brain that can understand such lasting kindness and care is the brain's attachment system.[7]

When we seek oneness with one another without realising that attachment is key, we don't live as family.

For both He who sanctifies and those who are sanctified are all from one Father; for this reason He is not ashamed to call them brothers and sisters,

Hebrews 2:11

Peter understood that followers of Jesus are the family of God. We are bound together as brothers and sisters.

Honour all people, love the brotherhood, fear God, honour the king.

So resist him, firm in your faith, knowing that the same experiences of suffering are being accomplished by your brothers and sisters who are in the world.

1 Peter 2:17; 5:9

So, if we forsake our pursuit of oneness with each other, we are abandoning to some degree our love for Jesus.

Families build lasting kindness and care that fosters attachment through identification with the same values. They create a set of norms that they sign up to as they pursue love and oneness with one another. In the Sermon on the Mount, Jesus shows how His kind of people will be known. They are people who take God's commands seriously; reconcile with others as a priority; have a high commitment to expressing their sexuality the way God intended; are faithful in marriage; allow their word to be their bond; look for God's perspective, not man's; and forgive knowing they are forgiven by Jesus.

So, with all that said, how can we apply this practically? What can we diligently practice so that we take every opportunity to love others through the way we see them? Here are some thoughts:

---

7   Hendricks. M., & Wilder. J., Op.cit. pg 81-82

CHAPTER 3

1. Practise being prepared to acknowledge when you have been offended so that you can find a way to embrace mercy instead. As you embrace mercy, pursue a process of discovery. Step away from the certainty of your conclusions based on limited knowledge. Allow discovery to guide the practice of asking questions. Resist the certainty of your conclusions being expressed through assertive statements.

2. Practise recognising your motivations that cause you to value characteristics that others don't. For example, if you are flexible and unstructured, you may feel restricted, restrained, or pressured when engaging with a more structured or rigid person. (Note that feelings are real but do not necessarily reflect the truth.)

3. Practise checking with others that what you heard is what was actually said. For example, you may hear a statement as criticism, whereas the intention may have been to help or encourage.

4. Practise balancing autonomy and accountability. Being free to express yourself may require accountability in considering the impact on others. The key here is mutual submission that is committed to the value of knowing and being known. Try to see from the other person's perspective.

5. Practise reminding yourself what kind of person reveals the Kingdom of God. Recognise that pursuing oneness with others is costly, as it often requires dying to your 'messed up' perceptions.

> The three friends who had been staring at her, now looked at Lom. On his face was an expression of such softness that Red could hardly bear it.
>
> Mrs Sider took a breath and turned to the three boys. 'I've heard…you laughing…at me but I've…never…smoked,' she whispered, 'it's mesothelioma…this thing I've got.' She swayed on her feet, exhausted by the effort to communicate. Lom offered her his arm, which she accepted gratefully. Red watched as they made their way slowly back to the house, stopping briefly at the garden bed for Lom to show her the crimson orchid. Her face crinkled with delight. Red thought back over the months they'd been coming to her house; the jokes at her expense; the silly pranks they'd gone back at night to play, like knocking on the door and running away. He imagined the effort it would have taken her to even make it to the door, only to find no-one there. But it was the judgement that she'd brought her sickness on herself that bothered him the most. They'd assumed something that simply wasn't true.

Something that justified their lack of compassion. Then there was Lom. Lom who'd stood there calmly trying to understand Red's issues with him, when red didn't even understand them himself. Red realised he knew very little about First Nations culture. Once again, he was sure he'd made assumptions that weren't true. But it was more than that. Lom's enthusiasm for restoring the garden and his kindness towards a vulnerable old lady, showed him to be the kind of person that Red secretly wished he himself was. A Jesus kind of person.

That night, Red rang Pastor Dom. It was embarrassing and awkward but he needed to tell her what had happened that day. She acknowledged the courage it took for him to be vulnerable and own his stuff. She asked him to tell her his story of growing up in his family and how he felt about himself. Red appreciated her patience and skill as she drew out of him his fears of being taken advantage of and of not being good enough. She explained how his attitudes were a defence. She talked about the human need for belonging, significance and security. Red began to understand that the process he was going through was happening exactly as God intended – within community. Red wasn't a failure. He was becoming more like Jesus. This thought led him back to Lom.

WHAT WE KNOW ABOUT OURSELVES

The third target for weapons that are designed to rob, steal and destroy the life of God is: what we know about ourselves.

We will never be able to find true oneness with others if we ignore what needs to change in our emotions.

Time for a short theological conversation about our 'self' that has profound consequences. So, stay with me - closely! Don't switch off.

Romans 6:6 speaks of the 'old self'.

> *knowing this, that our old self was crucified with Him, in order that our body of sin might be done away with, so that we would no longer be slaves to sin;*

The old self has been crucified. That is, the person I used to be in Adam, my old humanity born under the law, and my motivation, nature and personality governed by sin have died. Because of my union with Christ, my old self has died and been buried. I am now dead to sin as a realm and as a ruler. I have finished with it. It is nothing to me. It is now not my nature.

And yet, Ephesians 4:22 also speaks of the 'old self':

> *that, in reference to your former way of life, you are to rid yourselves of the old self, which is being corrupted in accordance with the lusts of deceit,*

If the old self is dead, how can I still be putting it off? The old self in Ephesians 4 is the flesh, the members of my body. It refers to conversations, conduct and behaviour that are CHARACTERISTIC of the old self. Sin is still in my instincts, propensities, drives, urges and powers of my body. That is: my hunger can lead to gluttony; my tongue can lead to gossip and strife; my mind can lead to sloth, greed and anger; and my sex drive can lead to lust. All have been affected by sin. All have 'muscle memory' so that they can govern me. Hence, Paul concludes:

> *and that you are to be renewed in the spirit of your minds, and to put on the new self, which in the likeness of God has been created in righteousness and holiness of the truth.*
>
> Eph. 4:23-24

The old self, the old man, is dead. However, the flesh is in process. Again, Paul writes:

> *For the law of the Spirit of life in Christ Jesus has set you free from the law of sin and of death.*
> *For the mind set on the flesh is death, but the mind set on the Spirit is life and peace,*
> *If Christ is in you, though the body is dead because of sin, yet the spirit is alive because of righteousness.*
> *For if you are living in accord with the flesh, you are going to die; but if by the Spirit you are putting to death the deeds of the body, you will live.*
> Rom. 8:2,6,10,13

The Spirit wants to help us recognise and understand our emotions. He wants us to be children of God through the awareness He brings to manage our behaviour and relationships. The Spirit is our counsellor, helper and comforter as we navigate social complexities and make personal decisions that lead to oneness with others.

Self-awareness comes from desiring a straightforward and honest understanding of what makes me tick. Personal responsibility is what happens when I act so that I remain flexible and direct my behaviour positively. Social awareness is the capacity to accurately pick up on the emotions of others and understand what is really going on for them. Relationship management is my ability to engage my awareness to manage interactions successfully. Psychological literature calls this emotional intelligence.

The reality is that we are all messed up. Being messed up means we are all challenged in our pursuit of being one with others. Brene Brown captures this truth when she writes:

> A deep sense of love and belonging is an irreducible need of all people. We are biologically, cognitively, physically, and spiritually wired to love, to be loved, and to belong. When those needs are not met, we don't function as we were meant to. We break. We fall apart. We numb. We ache. We hurt others. We get sick.[8]

I have discovered that we all want to belong, be significant and be secure. These three desires drive human needs we all live with and manage from the time we are born.

From an early age and throughout our lives, we endeavour to meet these needs by answering the question: what is right and required for acceptance? We ask this question in the context of the family or significant others we grow up with, our schooling experiences, where we engage in sporting or creative pursuits, in our workplaces, where we socialise, where we pursue our faith or spiritual journey; and many other social contexts.

Invariably, our answers are performance-based and tied to the cultural and institutional expectations of the group. This performance base results in 'counsellors of fear' in our self-talk. We are fearful of not being what is expected with the outcome of not belonging, being insignificant or insecure. From here, we learn how to defend and protect ourselves through being self-centred and self-reliant. We endeavour to control our world and exert personal power at the expense of others.

One of the reasons we stumble in our pursuit of oneness with others is that we are all messed up somehow by this dynamic. Henri Nouwen[9] expresses it this way:

> First, we have difficulty because of our intense need to be justified, a need rooted in our craving to be liked and accepted by the

---

8   Brown. B., (2010). *The Gifts of Imperfection*, Hazelden Information & Educational Services. Quote accessed via Good Reads. Retrieved on 3rd September 2021 from https://www.goodreads.com/author/quotes/162578.Bren_Brown?page=6
9   Nouwen, H., *Turning My Mourning Into Dancing... Finding Hope in Hard Times*, Thomas Nelson Publishers, Nashville 2001, pg 72-74

significant people in our lives… Second, we end up doing things for others for the sake of doing, for the sake of ourselves… ultimately placing our own unmet longings at the centre of our efforts… Third, our competitiveness…We do this so much that we even sometimes form our identities in comparison to others; we certainly never completely admit the possibility of giving up our sense of difference, of entering where others are weak, of sharing with another's pain. We have too much of ourselves and our ambitions to defend to easily allow that.

What we fear controls us. It makes idols of expectations. We live with the cry of: 'embrace me, value me, notice me and don't hurt me or abandon me.' All of these needs God is ready to meet through the revelation that we are: chosen (we belong), holy (we are significant), and beloved (we are secure) so that we begin to live powerfully in oneness with one another.

> *Therefore, as God's chosen people, holy and dearly loved, clothe yourselves with compassion, kindness, humility, gentleness and patience. Bear with each other and forgive one another if any of you has a grievance against someone. Forgive as the Lord forgave you. And over all these virtues, put on love, which binds them all together in perfect unity.*
>
> Colossians 3:12-14

Relationships are never perfect. However, if we are prepared to pursue the constant effort of personal transformation, we experience the healing of hurts and fractures endemic to human hearts. In this context, the true burden is bearing with one another. We show mercy and grace. We overlook offence. We forgive. We have no illusions or pipe dreams about our own wholeness or that of others. We become powerful contributors to true Christian community.

Henri Nouwen[10] provides the following insights to help illustrate what we face in choosing this road of personal transformation:

> This is not easy, of course, largely because of the ways we continue to crave attention, affection, influence, power, even after hearing God's word that we are his beloved. These needs are born from our wounds and never seem to be satisfied. When we try to find an explanation for these wounds, we discover how they have been inflicted on us by people who are needy people themselves. Through

---
10 Ibid, pg 87

the generations there seems to run a chain of wounds and needs. And when we try to avoid inflicting wounds ourselves, we discover that even with our best intentions we cannot avoid encountering people who feel rejected, misunderstood or hurt by us.

The impact of these thoughts on our oneness with others can be ascertained when we honestly ask ourselves: how fully am I devoted to others in brotherly love, and am I loyal regardless of any experience of tension and conflict with others?

Devotion and loyalty to others are deeply impacted by where we 'abide'.

> *Just as the Father has loved Me, I also have loved you; remain in My love. If you keep My commandments, you will remain in My love; just as I have kept My Father's commandments and remain in His love. These things I have spoken to you so that My joy may be in you, and that your joy may be made full.*
>
> John 15:9-11

The word 'abide' means to remain in. Jesus exhorts us to remain in His love through keeping His commandments so that His joy may be in us and our joy be made full.

Let's break this down.

Most followers of Jesus in the western world hear the word commandment as 'a statement of rules and regulations'. They perceive that God requires us to follow the rules and perform correctly to be blessed and avoid punishment. Right standing with God dominates and overshadows the place of right relationship.

The commandments of Jesus reveal God's original intent for relationship with Him and others. The commandments express Kingdom based love that is a decision of the heart to delight in another and to will their good ahead of their own. A love that is redemptive in purpose, nature, and outworking, believing there was original intent for relationships. This love does not come to us naturally.

Our natural tendency is to be self-centred and self-reliant. These are the places we naturally abide due to the conversations, conduct or behaviour that are characteristic of the old self. We are learning to put these off. That is not to remain or abide in them. Our guide in this process is to understand and pursue God's original intent in how to express love.

Again, the word 'keep' here actually means 'to protect'. An approach to relationship with God based on following the rules hears the word keep as 'obey'. Obey can engender the idea of self-effort for the purpose of reward. However, when we are motivated by a decision of the heart to delight in God, we will pursue protecting what is important to Him. That is, we adopt a posture of honouring the Father's place, position and authority beyond the exercise of our own perspective.

When we 'keep commandments' from this perspective, we are abiding in love. Jesus' commandments reveal God's best way to live with one another. They reveal His original intent. In relying on the Word, the Spirit and accountability in community, we are reaching into a redemptive process and learning to put on the new self.

There is a price to be paid to abide in Jesus' love. The price is to surrender our life to the truth that God knows best. The result is that change is required. Equally, the price includes trusting God in the process. This means we must accept that time is required. However, if we are prepared to pay the price, there is a prize on offer. The prize in John 15:11 is that Jesus' joy fills us, and our joy is full. There is also another prize for protecting God's commandments. We experience the delight and joy of the Father revealing to us who He really is: kind, good, faithful, merciful, powerful and much more.

> *The one who has My commandments and keeps them is the one who loves Me; and the one who loves Me will be loved by My Father, and I will love him and will reveal Myself to him."*
>
> John 14:21

At this point, what intrigues me is the discoveries from neuroscience of the crucial part joy plays in our relational development. Wilder and Hendricks write:

> When we are the sparkle in someone's eyes, their face lights up with a smile when they see us. We feel joy. From the moment we are born, joy shapes the chemistry, structure and growth of our brain. Joy lays the foundation for how well we will handle relationships, emotions, pain and pleasure throughout our lifetime. Joy creates an identity that is stable and consistent over time. Joy gives us the freedom to share our hearts with God and others. Expressing our joyful identity creates space for others to belong. Joy gives us the freedom to live without masks because, in spite of our weaknesses, we know we are loved. We are not afraid of our vulnerabilities or exposure. Joy gives us the

freedom from fear to live from the heart Jesus gave us. We discover increasing delight in becoming the people God knew we could be.[11]

God designed our brains to run on joy as a car runs on fuel. Our brains desire joy more than any other thing. God's presence is connected with joy:

> *You will make known to me the way of life;*
> *In Your presence is fullness of joy;*
> *In Your right hand there are pleasures forever.*
>
> Psalm 16:11
>
> *For You make him [most blessed forever;*
> *You make him joyful with the joy of Your presence.*
>
> Psalm 21:6

The original Hebrew can be translated to replace 'Your presence' with 'Your face' in both these verses.

Wilder and Hendricks write:

> God designed our brains to seek joy through eyes and facial expressions, through being with people who are glad to be with us. When I compared the many Scriptures that describe God's face shining on us with what I now know about how our brains were designed, I came to three important points of convergence: (1) Joy is primarily transmitted through the face (especially the eyes) and secondarily through voice. (2) Joy is relational. It is what we feel when we are with someone who is happy to be with us. Joy does not exist outside of a relationship. (3) Joy is important to God and to us.
>
> Reading through the Bible and replacing "joy" with the concept of God's face lighting up gives us a better idea of what joy means. In John 15, Jesus talks about how He loves His disciples with the same love that the Father has for Him. Then He says, "I have told you this so that my joy may be in you and that your joy may be complete"(v 11). If we replace "joy" with the fuller definition, Jesus' statement would be, "My Father's face lights up when He sees Me because I'm so special to Him. I'm telling you this so that you will feel how special you are to my Father and to Me. Our faces are shining on you with delight.[12]

---

11 Hendricks. M., & Wilder. J., Op. cit. pg 61&62
12 Ibid, pg 56 & 57

Our devotion and loyalty to others are deeply impacted by where we abide. When we abide in Jesus' love, through keeping (protecting) His commandments (original intent), we receive His joy. His joy helps in the process of reshaping our identity around who we are in Christ. His joy reshapes the foundations from which we manage our relationships with one another. His joy helps us put off self-centred emotions and pain that undermine our pursuit of wanting the good of others ahead of our own.

Our devotion and loyalty to others are empowered by our commitment to encourage one another.

Jesus is the great encourager. We are constantly being called up into our righteousness in the Holy Spirit.

> *and regarding righteousness, because I am going to the Father and you no longer are going to see Me;*

John 16:10

The Father, Jesus, and Holy Spirit speak hope, potential and redemptive opportunities into who we are. They are restoring us to the way God originally intended us to be. They release divine destiny to us, moulding us into their image.

> *For those whom He foreknew, He also predestined to become conformed to the image of His Son, so that He would be the firstborn among many brothers and sisters;*

Rom. 8:29

We are called to be the same for those around us. We are to affirm, encourage and speak prophetically to one another. We are to strengthen others with comfort, strength and inspiration.

> *not abandoning our own meeting together, as is the habit of some people, but encouraging one another; and all the more as you see the day drawing near.*

Heb. 10:25

Scripture reveals numerous ways we can encourage one another.

Through our words:

> *Therefore, comfort one another with these words.*

1 Thess. 4:18

Judas and Silas, also being prophets themselves, encouraged and strengthened the brothers and sisters with a lengthy message.

Acts 15:32

By offering to support others in practical ways, being reliable and a faithful friend.

Bear one another's burdens, and thereby fulfil the law of Christ.

Gal.6:2

By going the extra mile with those who carry low self-esteem and are rebuilding from very broken foundations.

*We urge you, brothers **and sisters**, admonish the unruly, encourage the fainthearted, help the weak, be patient with everyone.*

1 Thess. 5:14

Here are some thoughts on what to diligently practise so that you take every opportunity to love others through growing in what we know about ourselves.

1. Practise giving yourself space to find God's 'love zone' for you when you are tempted to throw a tantrum. Through self-awareness and personal responsibility, step into a redemptive process. Reach for grace and revelation to be restored back to the love of the Kingdom.

2. Practise exploring the mystery of love that pays a cost for the benefit of others. Stop practising the establishment of certainty that is pursued in 'being right' and standing in judgement.

3. Practise vulnerability and transparency with others you have built trust with, knowing that the light found in a loving community will lead to untangling the sin and the doubt that we wrestle with.

4. Practice being open and honest in trusting relationships about your fears, discouragement and failures. Sharing weakness is an apostolic way of life. (1 Cor. 2:3, 2 Cor. 11:30)

5. Practise being teachable. The capacity to hear and reflect on feedback from those who are committed to your welfare and future will enable you to flourish.

CHAPTER 3

SUMMARY

— What we practise affects what we inherit.

— Be led by the Spirit in your diligent practice of expressing love and devotion to others.

— When you are squeezed by life, and you don't express 'Jesus juice', choose self-awareness and personal responsibility to enter a transformation process.

— We are loved by the Father in the same way the Father loves Jesus.

— Stop. Look. Listen.

— Pursue Spirit-filled faithfulness in a culture overrun with allegiance to self.

— How we love one another reveals how much we know God.

— How we see someone impacts how we treat them.

— We will never be able to find true oneness with others if we ignore what needs to change in our emotions.

QUESTIONS AND ACTIVITIES

1. Name two practices from this chapter you are prepared to commit to diligently pursue over the next six months.

2. When you are squeezed by life, which two of your regular expressions of 'self' will you ask the Holy Spirit to help you change?

3. Which three STOP. LOOK. LISTEN practices will you focus on orientating yourself towards over the next six months?

4. Who could you trust to be open with to explore through prayer and accountability an area of weakness in how you love others?

Chapter 4

A Call to Transformation

...How To Abide in Love.

- We have a sacred duty to live brilliantly with one another
- The sacred duty is empowered by abiding in love
- There are five values to be lived through to abide in love
  - Shalom, righteousness, relational faithfulness, what love requires and trust
- To become whole in living through these values is necessary for:
  - Shalom to increase through changed perspectives
  - Righteousness to flourish through soul keeping
  - Relational faithfulness to be anchored in joy
  - What love requires to be reviewed in light of commandments
  - Trust to find expression in the context of suffering.

Abiding in love in the context of community is deeply challenging. The challenges can be attributed to the failings of others. However, in nearly four decades of pastoring, I have found that a Kingdom response begins with paying attention to my contribution. Allow me to illustrate with this teaching by me to the community I have served for over thirty years - Stairway Church.

> Thanks for taking the time to join me as you listen to my reflections on pursuing and maintaining oneness with each other. I have decided to bring this teaching to help anyone in the Stairway community who was being unsettled by some emerging disruptive influences. I want to help us all understand the kingdom and biblical response when we carry or hear of possible grievances that result in gossip, rumours and/or third-party offences. A third-party offence is where we come to the defence of others when we feel they have been aggrieved. When we only know one side of the story. It is not my intent to address the content of any grievances, gossip, rumours or third-party offences. Rather, I am concerned that we all manage ourselves through biblical expectations that pursue oneness and avoid division. Ephesians 4:1-3 is helpful to remember at this point:
>
>> *Therefore, I, the prisoner of the Lord implore you to walk in a manner worthy of the calling with which you have been called.*
>
> So, just to create a little bit of context here, *worthy of the calling* refers to the first three chapters. The calling in the first three chapters is all about our oneness with God, our oneness with one another, and how to grow in our oneness with God and our oneness with one another. So, Paul is imploring us to walk in a manner worthy of the calling of pursuing oneness with God and oneness with one another.
>
> Verse 2 states:
>
>> *With all humility and gentleness, with patience, showing tolerance for one another in love, being diligent to preserve the unity of the spirit in the bond of peace.*
>
> As we come to reflect on these ideas today, I want to now read from Matthew 6:33
>
>> *But seek first His kingdom and His righteousness, and all these things will be added to you.*

In the context of possible grievances, gossip, rumour and third-party offence, what does it look like to seek His kingdom and His righteousness?

First of all, to seek His kingdom in this context, we need to turn to Jesus' teaching, which is very clear. We see this in Matthew 18:15

> *If your brother sins, go show him his fault in private between you and him alone. If he listens to you, you have won your brother.*

When Adam and Eve sinned against the Father, He entered the garden to show them their error through the process of discovery. He asked them two questions, trying to understand their perspective. The two questions were: "Where are you" and "Who told you that?" The Father's approach in private was characterised by humility, inquiry, and a need to hear events from their perspective. The mistake Adam and Eve made was that they listened to the accuser challenge the character of their Father, the one who loved them the most. They didn't go to their Father and say, "This is what we have been told. Can you help us understand?"

When grievance, gossip, rumour and third-party offences are rooted in accusation, it can only be demonically inspired. The devil's approach is based in accusation characterised by pride, being right, and one-sided in its certainty. To seek the kingdom in the context of grievance, gossip, rumour, and third-party offence is to go to the one who you think has sinned and like the Father, ask questions in humility to hear their perspective before doing anything else. Let's always remember that there are at least two sides to every story. If we have missed this step and have adopted a posture of accusation, then to return to the ways of the kingdom requires humility to repent. This repentance is then expressed through going in private, with a heart of inquiry and discovery to hear the perspective of the side of the story that hasn't been heard yet.

> To live in the kingdom and to seek the kingdom in this instance is not to stay in accusation, partner with accusation, or assume you know what has taken place. Equally, participating in gossip or spreading rumours will only increase the circle of offence that has come from the accusation based on incomplete or misleading informa-

tion. A kingdom response is to go to all we have gossiped with or spread the rumours to repent of our actions, and together attempt to hear the other side of the story which has not been heard and to stop talking about what we don't really know.

To seek righteousness in the context of grievances, gossip, rumours, and third-party offences begins in 2 Corinthians 5:21:

He made Him who knew no sin to be sin on our behalf so that we might become the righteousness of God in Him.

There are two aspects of righteousness. The first is propitiation. Propitiation means the penalty that was required to pay for sin so that we can have right standing with God. The second aspect of righteousness is expiation. This is the removal of sin so that we can be in right relationship with God. We have right standing with God and can live in right relationship with God because God was faithful to His relationship with mankind. That is, He was faithful to His promise in Genesis 3, to provide a way back into the family of God and for us to be His children. He was faithful to the relationship because He is love.

The New Testament commandment is "Love one another as I have loved you." The New Testament commandment calls us to seek, through love, to be faithful to all our relationships and to pursue courses of redemption and reconciliation. The New Testament commandment calls us to seek to live in right relationship with others by walking in a manner worthy of our calling. The New Testament commandment calls us to seek righteousness in our relationships by being diligent to preserve the unity of the Spirit in peace.

Paul saw this as a sacred duty. In Ephesians 5:21, he writes:

Be subject to one another in the fear or reverence of Christ.

And so, for Paul, we are meant to be subject to one another from a place of awe of who we are in Christ. It is a sacred call upon our lives. It is not a choice we get to make if we want to follow Jesus in the New Testament commandment of loving one another as He has loved us.

Therefore, in the context of grievance, gossip, rumour and third-party offence, we are to be guided by three principles: to seek reconciliation through love; to be faithful to all of our relationships; to seek to live in right relationship with others and to pursue righteousness in our relationships. These principles are summarised in Ephesians 4:31-32:

> *Let all bitterness and wrath and anger be put away from you along with all malice. Be kind to one another, tender-hearted, forgiving each other, just as God in Christ also has forgiven you.*

I will be the first to recognise that the Stairway community is not perfect. I will acknowledge that I make mistakes, and I am on a lifelong journey toward everything in my heart being restored to the way God originally intended it to be. We are served by a wonderful team of leaders who continually bring their best selves to serve us all well. However, when relationships come under pressure and scrutiny, can I invite you to be one who seeks first the Kingdom of God and His righteousness? That is, honour those who are the subject of grievances, gossip, rumour or third-party offence by approaching them personally with a heart of inquiry or simply don't say anything to anyone that you are not sure about. Secondly, if after inquiry you are not satisfied, keep following Jesus' model in Matthew 18, through a heart of love, not punishment. Be faithful to the relationship, and as much as it depends on you, stay in right relationship. Finally, if after inquiry you are satisfied, extend forgiveness to the one that you judged and let any offence go.

The Stairway community is a gift from God. The Stairway community is a church that the Lord established. It is full of people who are genuinely trying to love God and love one another. At this time, we are under significant spiritual influence to step away from our commitment to Relentless Love, and we need together to encourage one another to stay the course of Relentless Love. That is my prayer for all of us today.

> So let me finish by praying. I ask, Holy Spirit, that you would help me and every other member of Stairway Church to live in right relationship with one another. That we would be faithful to the relationships, you have established, and we would be faithful to your principles. And that, Father, where we bump into grievance, gossip,

rumours or third-party offence, that we would look at how You want us to conduct ourselves. Help us to help others know how to conduct themselves. And Father, that we would not enter anything that is divisive, that is accusatory, or that is going to bring damage. Lord, I ask for Your grace and Your help at this time as we learn together to stand in love and believe the best of one another while still having what can be, at times, tough conversations to establish what it is that we really need to know. I ask all of this in Jesus' name. Amen.

God bless you. I trust that this has been helpful for you today and look forward to continuing to walk into a bright future together.

A SACRED DUTY

Living in oneness with one another isn't just a nice idea; it is a sacred call and duty.

> *...and subject yourselves to one another in the fear of Christ.*
>
> Eph.5:21
>
> *...so we, who are many, are one body in Christ, and individually parts of one another.*
>
> Rom. 12:5

To live in oneness is expressing our reverence for Jesus through a commitment to being subject to one another. It is adopting a counter-cultural position to individualism and embracing the wonder of mutual submission through righteousness. Henri Nouwen expresses it this way:

> Jesus calls us to seek our unity in and through Him. When we direct our inner attention not first of all to each other, but to God to whom we belong, then we will discover that in God we also belong to each other.[1]

As we surrender our will to God, we love people from a place of being surrendered to love itself. Therefore, it makes sense to say that if I bring about a division in the fabric of someone's relationships, I am abandoning the sacred call and duty to be surrendered to love itself. To loving that person as Jesus does.

1 Nouwen. H., (2020, July 28). The Divine Gift of Unity, *Henri Nouwen Society*, https://henrinouwen.org/meditation/the-divine-gift-of-unity/

As you will have seen by now, after recognising a truth, I go to questions to discover the depths of that truth and how to apply it to my life. So, the questions here are: What is required of me to fulfil this sacred call and duty? What values do I need to hold to abide in love? What does it look like day to day to be one who joins a web of stubbornly loyal relationships, knitted together in a living network of persons, committed to practising the ways of Jesus together for the renewal of the world?

SHALOM

The first value to hold on to to abide in love is shalom. Jesus came to establish His Kingdom. A Kingdom where shalom is a central value and reality; where Jesus has come to heal all that is wrong with the world; and the focus is to restore everything back to the way God originally intended it to be.

> *"These things I have spoken to you while remaining with you. But the Helper, the Holy Spirit whom the Father will send in My name, He will teach you all things, and remind you of all that I said to you. Peace I leave you, My peace I give you; not as the world gives, do I give to you. Do not let your hearts be troubled, nor fearful."*
>
> John 14:25-27

The experience of shalom is multi-dimensional, and its meaning rich and multi-faceted. Fundamentally, shalom means reconciliation with God. Reconciliation leads to the possibility of a flourishing life through restoration, harmony, wholeness, completeness, prosperity, welfare and tranquillity. Shalom is revealed as the reconciliation of all things to God through the work of Christ (Col. 1:19-20). It flows from all our relationships being put right. It leads to an experience of inner security that brings a profound and complete experience of well-being – physically, psychologically, socially and spiritually.

Sadly, Shalom is often not our reality. Shalom speaks of reconciliation, yet we live with separation. Shalom releases flourishing while we live with frustration. Shalom promotes living networks of people, yet we are faced with isolation and brokenness. Shalom is often not our reality because we live with inner turmoil.

> *Jesus replied to them, "Do you now believe? Behold, an hour is coming, and has already come, for you to be scattered, each to his own home, and to leave Me alone; and yet I am not alone, because the Father is with Me. These things I have spoken to you so that in Me you may*

> have peace. In the world you have tribulation, but take courage; I have overcome the world."

John 16:31-33

The word 'tribulation' here means inner turmoil, which can be described as the areas in our hearts where anxiety, fear, doubt and unbelief reside. Jesus is about to experience being deserted by His closest friends in His greatest hour of need. Their desertion will create an environment where most of us would experience abandonment, loss and rejection. When we engage with these experiences through our places of inner turmoil, we feel alone. Yet Jesus is declaring that because He lives in Shalom with the Father, He does not experience being alone. Jesus is offering us the opportunity to exchange our inner turmoil for His peace. Our tribulation for His shalom. This shalom garrisons our hearts against anxiety, difficulties and sorrows (Phil. 4:4-7). We find a peace so deep we can be content in times of great challenge (Phil.4:12-13).

The opportunity to exchange our inner turmoil is an invitation to experience transformation.

> *Now may the God of peace Himself sanctify you entirely; and may your spirit and soul and body be kept complete, without blame at the coming of our Lord Jesus Christ.*

1 Thess. 5:23

RIGHTEOUSNESS

The second value to hold on to to abide in love is righteousness, which, as already discussed, has two meanings: right standing and right relationship.

We are called to practise righteousness.

> *Little children, make sure no one deceives you; the one who practices righteousness is righteous, just as He is righteous; the one who practices sin is of the devil; for the devil has been sinning from the beginning. The Son of God appeared for this purpose, to destroy the works of the devil.*

1 John 3:7-8

Our right standing with God is positional. We have been made righteous and are holy, blameless and beyond reproach. However, this is not our daily experience as we fall short of living in the fullness of what we have inherited. So, to practise righteousness is to practise being in right relationship. Right relationship with God, self and others.

We are called to seek righteousness.

> *But seek first His kingdom and His righteousness, and all these things will be provided to you.*
>
> Matt.6:33

When we seek righteousness, we are seeking to be in right relationship with God, self and others. We are pursuing the qualities of a relationship that marks us as being like God in the way we love: qualities of humility; forgiveness; servanthood; honour; devotion with respect; patience; and, kindness. This is what we are to practice and seek.

The Holy Spirit convicts us of righteousness.

> *and regarding righteousness, because I am going to the Father and you no longer are going to see Me;*
>
> John 16:10

The Holy Spirit is committed to helping us be conformed to the image of Jesus.

Consequently, He will lead us to see the behaviour, attitudes and self-talk that leads us into unrighteousness, so that we can repent and turn towards Him. The Holy Spirit longs that we would experience the freedom Jesus won for us. Freedom from the lies that inform our choices to participate in ways of living that break, damage and undermine being one with others. Proverbs is helpful here:

> *There are six things that the Lord hates,*
> *Seven that are an abomination to Him:*
> *Haughty eyes, a lying tongue,*
> *And hands that shed innocent blood,*
> *A heart that devises wicked plans,*
> *Feet that run rapidly to evil,*
> *A false witness who declares lies,*
> *And one who spreads strife among brothers.*
>
> Proverbs 6:16-19

> *One who declares truth tells what is right,*
> *But a false witness, deceit.*
> *There is one who speaks rashly like the thrusts of a sword,*
> *But the tongue of the wise brings healing.*
> *Truthful lips will endure forever,*
> *But a lying tongue is only for a moment.*
> *Deceit is in the heart of those who devise evil,*
> *But counsellors of peace have joy.*
> *No harm happens to the righteous,*
> *But the wicked are filled with trouble.*
> *Lying lips are an abomination to the Lord,*
> *But those who deal faithfully are His delight.*
>
> Proverbs 12:17-22

The Holy Spirit works to free us to love one another as Jesus has loved us.

Pursuing right relationship with God is empowered by a lifestyle of humility and surrender to the supreme rule and reign of Jesus' authority. Pursuing right relationship with ourselves is empowered by working out our salvation in knowing our identity in Christ. We are holy, chosen and beloved and not subject or enslaved to fear. Pursuing right relationship with others is empowered by being diligent in preserving the unity of the Spirit in the bond of peace (Eph. 4:3). This includes only offering personal opinions that give value to others.[2] It is enhanced by offering commentary and observations, not criticism and judgement, to disciple people away from the consequences of acting out of their inner turmoil. This is powerfully illustrated in Peter's experience as Jesus restored right relationship to him.

Peter's inner turmoil resulted in him denying Jesus three times. He broke right relationship with Jesus and himself.

> *And then the Lord turned and looked at Peter. And Peter remembered the word of the Lord, how He had told him, "Before a rooster crows today, you will deny Me three times." And he went out and wept bitterly.*
>
> Luke 22:61-62

Jesus is fully committed to righteous behaviour and so restored relationship with Peter and returned Peter back to himself through love.

---

[2] John 17:22, "The glory which You have given Me…" Here the word 'glory' means 'to offer a personal opinion that gives value.'

CHAPTER 4

Now when they had finished breakfast, Jesus said to Simon Peter, "Simon, son of John, do you love Me more than these?" He said to Him, "Yes, Lord; You know that I love You." He said to him, "Tend My lambs." He said to him again, a second time, "Simon, son of John, do you love Me?" He said to Him, "Yes, Lord; You know that I love You." He said to him, "Shepherd My sheep." He said to him the third time, "Simon, son of John, do you love Me?" Peter was hurt because He said to him the third time, "Do you love Me?" And he said to Him, "Lord, You know all things; You know that I love You." Jesus said to him, "Tend My sheep.

John 21:15-17

The opportunity to grow in righteousness and live in the right relationship with God, self, and others is an invitation to experience transformation.

"Blessed are those who hunger and thirst for righteousness, for they will be satisfied".

Matt. 5:6

RELATIONAL FAITHFULNESS

The third value to hold to to abide in love is relational faithfulness.

God's love and forgiveness are based in His faithfulness to relationship with all mankind. He was faithful in providing, through Jesus, a way to restore us to the family of God. The Lord's faithfulness to relationship is founded in His deep and abiding love for mankind. God's example of faithfulness to relationship is expressed in Christian community through mutual submission and the reality that we are all members of one another.

Do nothing from selfishness or empty conceit, but with humility consider one another as more important than yourselves;

Phil. 2:3

You younger men, likewise, be subject to your elders; and all of you, clothe yourselves with humility toward one another, because God is opposed to the proud, but He gives grace to the humble.

1 Peter 5:5

> *so we, who are many, are one body in Christ, and individually parts of one another.*
>
> Rom. 12:5

Faithfulness can be translated as both steadfast love and lovingkindness. It carries a sense of enduring connection that brings life and all good things into a relationship. It is the kind and loyal care for the well-being of another. This is the kind of community Jesus came to establish, a *hesed* community, one that is focused on kindness and loyal care for the well-being of others.

> *See how great a love the Father has given us, that we would be called children of God; and in fact we are. For this reason the world does not know us: because it did not know Him.*
>
> 1 John 3:1

As the Father lavishes His love on His children, we are a spiritual family glued together by that love.

> *Beloved, let's love one another; for love is from God, and everyone who loves has been born of God and knows God. The one who does not love does not know God, because God is love. By this the love of God was revealed in us, that God has sent His only Son into the world so that we may live through Him.*
>
> *Beloved, if God so loved us, we also ought to love one another. No one has ever seen God; if we love one another, God remains in us, and His love is perfected in us.*
>
> 1 John 4:7-9, 11-12

Our shared love, not our shared interests, holds us together in this spiritual family.

> *For both He who sanctifies and those who are sanctified are all from one Father; for this reason He is not ashamed to call them brothers and sisters,*
>
> Hebrews 2:11

In this context, Wilder and Hendricks[3] observe:

---

[3] Wilder, J & Henricks, M., op cit. pg 87

CHAPTER 4

In John 15, Jesus uses the analogy of a branch and vine to explain our relationship to Him and the Father:

"I am the vine: you are the branches. If you remain in me and I in you, you will bear much fruit; apart from me you can do nothing.....As the Father has loved me, so have I loved you. Now remain in my love... My command is this: Love each other as I have loved you." (vv. 5,9,12)

The image of a vine and branch is a clear picture of attachment. We have an attachment to Jesus that bears fruit in our lives (character change). He presents a simple formula: no attachment, no fruit. Through the Father's attachment to Jesus, divine love flows to us through our connection to the vine. Our attachment to Jesus does not dead-end. The flow of divine sap courses through our attachments to each other. We see the stream of God's love spreading spiritual nutrition through our *hesed* attachments, from top to bottom. Our character is transformed through this flow of love. A *hesed* community has the Father's love in its veins and is bursting with fruit.

Interestingly, in nature, autumn leaves change colour and die because the flow of sugar is blocked. That is, the lifeblood ceases to flow and be available. So, it is with our spiritual communities. Our individual connection to the vine releases God's friendship, attachment and love so that lovingkindness can flow. It is then that we can be faithful to our relationships. If our brokenness blocks this flow, then our faithfulness is undermined.

Our value for faithfulness to relationships needs to be a posture we adopt towards everyone.

All bitterness, wrath, anger, clamour, and slander must be removed from you, along with all malice. Be kind to one another, compassionate, forgiving each other, just as God in Christ also has forgiven you.

Eph. 4:31-32

The opportunity to grow in our faithfulness to relationships is an invitation to experience transformation.

As iron sharpens iron,
So one person sharpens another.

Proverbs 27:17

Faithful are the wounds of a friend,
But deceitful are the kisses of an enemy.

Proverbs 27:6

WHAT LOVE REQUIRES

The fourth value to hold to to abide in love is to always ask the question: what does love require?

Biblical love is redemptive in purpose, nature and outworking. It speaks to God's original intent in relationships. Biblical love is a decision of the heart to delight in another and to will their good ahead of your own.

To abide in this love and for love to flourish requires certain ingredients or environments; just like a plant, flourishing requires good soil, sunlight and water.

The first requirement or environment that we need to create for love to flourish is that we centre our spirituality and formation around the receiving and giving of loving devotion and attachment.

> *I am giving you a new commandment, that you love one another; just as I have loved you, that you also love one another.*
>
> John 13:34
>
> *and to know the love of Christ which surpasses knowledge, that you may be filled to all the fullness of God.*
>
> Eph. 3:19

As we centre our spirituality and formation in this way, we must return to the Word of God to guide our surrender to, and trust in, His ways.

> *The one who has My commandments and keeps them is the one who loves Me; and the one who loves Me will be loved by My Father, and I will love him and will reveal Myself to him."*
>
> John 14:21

We are commanded to live for the purpose of love. To fulfil this, we need to be transformed from our own knowledge of love; to enter a process so we can embrace and live out who we have become in Jesus.

CHAPTER 4

> *So then, my beloved, just as you have always obeyed, not as in my presence only, but now much more in my absence, work out your own salvation with fear and trembling; for it is God who is at work in you, both to desire and to work for His good pleasure.*

Phil. 2:12-13

The second requirement for love to flourish is found as we consider the place and power of imitation. Discipleship presupposes imitation.

> *It is enough for the disciple that he may become like his teacher, and the slave like his master. If they have called the head of the house Beelzebul, how much more will they insult the members of his household!*

Matt. 10:25

> *I am giving you a new commandment, that you love one another; just as I have loved you, that you also love one another.*

John 13:34

> *Be imitators of me, just as I also am of Christ.*

1 Cor. 11:1

When we choose to serve the good of another where there is tension, we lay down the right or need to serve our own purpose. John highlights this when he rightly observes that undisplayed love equals no love.

> *If someone says, "I love God," and yet he hates his brother or sister, he is a liar; for the one who does not love his brother and sister whom he has seen, cannot love God, whom he has not seen. And this commandment we have from Him, that the one who loves God must also love his brother and sister.*

1 John 4:20-21

As noted previously, the word 'hate' here means disregard, disrespect, or dismiss. This is such a natural human response to tension in a relationship. John declares that we are commanded by God in these situations to imitate Jesus. The word 'cannot' in verse 20 speaks to the idea of opportunity and ability. We don't love those we are in tension with when we choose not to take the opportunity to love like God loves. To have the ability to love as God does, we need to be transformed into being imitators of Jesus' love. This is the second requirement.

> *For those whom He foreknew, He also predestined to become conformed to the image of His Son, so that He would be the firstborn among many brothers and sisters;*

Rom. 8:29

The third requirement for love to flourish is an approach to life that protects loving God's way as the most precious thing.

> *This is His commandment, that we believe in the name of His Son Jesus Christ, and love one another, just as He commanded us. The one who keeps His commandments remains in Him, and He in him. We know by this that He remains in us, by the Spirit whom He has given us.*

1 John 3:23-24

The word 'keeps' in verse 23 means to protect. In this context, the meaning is not obey. Remember the illustration I gave in the last chapter of my response to someone trying to harm my family. I would do all in my power to protect them from that outcome. John is calling followers of Jesus to protect 'loving one another, as I have loved you' in this same way so that we abide in Him. When we judge others, prosecute our case and insist that we are right, we are not protecting love. We need to be transformed from judgement that scatters to love that gathers.

> *"You have heard that it was said, 'You shall love your neighbour and hate your enemy.' But I say to you, love your enemies and pray for those who persecute you, so that you may prove yourselves to be sons of your Father who is in heaven; for He causes His sun to rise on the evil and the good, and sends rain on the righteous and the unrighteous.*

Matt.5:43-45

TRUST

The fifth value to hold to to abide in love is trust. Vanessa Hall provides some beneficial insights regarding trust.[4] She suggests that we all build trust based on three core elements of expectations, needs and promises.

Expectations are something we all have a lot of that we don't necessarily communicate and are often unaware of. Over time, our brain tells us to plan for whatever we expect will happen. Some expectations are positive; many are negative.

---

[4] Hall. V., (2021). *The Ultimate Truth About Trust.* Entente Pty Ltd

Needs, again, are something that we all have and include the need for air, water and shelter; the need for safety and security; the need for love and belonging; the need for respect and confidence; and the need for growth and learning. We actively seek out people and things to meet our needs, and there are lots of places to look.

Promises are made by people and things that most align with what we expect and need. We choose to believe them, placing our fragile trust in their hands.

We have a free will to choose who we trust and to choose which promises we believe. However, our trust is often broken and betrayed. We become frustrated, disappointed, disillusioned and angry, resulting in judgement, aggression and self-centred activity to be safe or in control.

Throughout the Word of God, we are reminded to not trust in people and things but to put our trust in God. When we choose to trust fully in the promises of others to meet our expectations and needs, we forget our own spiritual nature. We are to trust God with our purpose, identity, relationships and lives. We do this in the knowledge that the Father loves us just as He loves Jesus. We are to align our expectations and needs to God's promises. We are called to trust what He has already promised.

We cannot love fully without placing our trust in God, who is in charge. Without this trust, we experience too much hurt and brokenness. From here, it is harder to forgive those who break our trust. If we are broken, bitter, or vengeful, it may simply mean that we trusted others too much.

The opportunity to grow in trusting God is an invitation to experience transformation.

> *Trust in the Lord with all your heart*
> *And do not lean on your own understanding.*
> *In all your ways acknowledge Him,*
> *And He will make your paths straight.*
>
> Prov. 3:5-6

BECOMING WHOLE

The values of shalom, righteousness, relational faithfulness, pursuing what love requires and trust lead us to abide in love. They are the foundations on which to build our sacred duty of living in oneness with one another. There are, however, things that will undermine our ability to do this. Primarily, it is our brokenness that undermines this sacred duty. To overcome this, we need to pursue transformation and spiritual formation to become whole and complete so as not to contribute to the chaos that relationships can bring. Like anything we are allowing Holy Spirit to help us overcome, personal transformation for the healing of inherent fractures that are endemic to human hearts requires perseverance. We need to learn to allow time and space to become our friends as we discover and celebrate the importance of process.

> *After you have suffered for a little while, the God of all grace, who called you to His eternal glory in Christ, will Himself perfect, confirm, strengthen, and establish you.*
>
> 1 Peter 5:10

There is a growing body of literature that successfully and with great breadth covers the need for spiritual formation. It provides a wide range of insights and practices that will greatly help your life with God as you become conformed to His image.

Peter Scazzaro[5] writes:

> What we are after is long term inner transformation into the image of Christ for the sake of the world; if you decide to set out on this path, you will most likely experience times of confusion, fear and grief; and, just because God has access to everything that is true about us does not mean God has access to us.

Dallas Willard[6] writes:

> The most important thing in your life is not what you do; it's who you become; the inner self must be changed; build a strategy for becoming the person God knows we ought to be; and, it is the inner life of the soul that we must aim to transform, and the behaviour will naturally follow.

John Ortberg[7] writes:

> One day, God will review with us what our souls have become, that is what will matter from our lives. I care for my soul because if

---

5 Scazzaro. P., (2015) *The Emotionally Healthy Leader*, Zondervan, Chapter 2 – Four Pathways for Facing Your Shadow (accessed via eBook, therefore no page number provided)
6 Willard. D., (1998) *The Divine Conspiracy*, William Collins, Chapter 5 (accessed via eBook, therefore no page numbers provided)
7 Ortberg. J., (2014). *Soul Keeping*, Zondervan, Chapter 7 (accessed via eBook, therefore no page numbers provided)

it becomes unhealthy, it will infect others. We have two worlds to manage: an outer world of career, possessions and social networks; and an inner world that is spiritual in nature, where values are selected and character is formed- a place where worship, confession and humility can be practised.

In the context of being one with God and one another Ephesians 3:14-19 indicates the need for formation and transformation: 'to be strengthened with power through His Spirit in the inner man.' This prayer creates the context for these uplifting yet often quoted out of context verses:

> *Now to Him who is able to do far more abundantly beyond all that we ask or think, according to the power that works within us, to Him be the glory in the church and in Christ Jesus to all generations forever and ever. Amen.*
>
> Eph. 3:20-21

God's exceeding abundance is for our transformation so the church in every generation would fulfil the sacred duty of oneness with one another.

Now that we have explored the values that form the foundation for abiding in love, the next question to ask becomes: how do we become whole in these values of shalom, righteousness, relational faithfulness, pursuing what love requires and trust?

> The next week, they gathered once again at Mrs Sider's. Red had taken the opportunity during the week to talk to Ant and Ving. They told him he was beating himself up for no reason. He knew they were trying to make him feel better, but he didn't want to feel better, he wanted to BE better. When Lom turned up, Red exhaled with relief. He'd been worried that Lom wouldn't show. He asked Lom if they could speak privately before they started work. Lom readily agreed. Red prayed as he'd been praying all week, inviting Holy Spirit to give him the words to say. He could see Ant and Ving craning their necks, trying to see what was happening but Red made sure he and Lom were well out of earshot.
>
> Red forced himself to look Lom in the eye. 'I... I need to say sorry for the way I,' Dom had encouraging him to name the wrong specifically, 'disrespected you, last week.' Red's insides roiled. The stakes felt impossibly high. It wasn't just about doing the right thing. He wanted Lom to give him another chance. But he knew, from talking to Dom, that even if Lom chose to forgive him, restoration of relationship was not automatic. In

fact, restoration wasn't possible, or even desirable, if the person was unsafe. Red never wanted to be an unsafe person for Lom to be around.

'Thanks for that. Not easy to do,' said Lom, and the warmth in his voice gave Red hope. When Lom held out his hand, Red grasped the forgiveness offered. This, right here, is what the kingdom is all about, thought Red. We're different but we're one. He hoped that given time Ant and Ving would catch on. He knew better than to preach to them. They needed to be convinced of Red's love for them, just as Lom did. He'd need to practice this kind of living in oneness. And Mrs Sider? Well, the Master Gardener had sent them to love her back to life, along with her garden. He would show them how.

SHALOM AND PERSPECTIVE

It has been said that 'sin is the vandalism of shalom'. Shalom, as we've explored, being reconciliation with God, harmony with ourselves and others, and an inner security that brings profound psychological and emotional well-being.

God's plan for mankind was always to live in oneness with Him where we were whole and complete. The enemy lied to Adam and Eve, saying that their oneness with God was inferior to the opportunity of being like God. They fell short in loving God when they sinned by eating the fruit of the tree of the knowledge of good and evil. Their falling short broke oneness with God, 'we were afraid of You'; broke oneness with themselves, 'I hid myself'; and broke oneness with one another, 'the woman who you gave me' is responsible.

Their sin resulted in separation now experienced in our brokenness and the vandalism of shalom.

In Christ, our oneness with God has been restored! We are holy, blameless, and beyond reproach; all our sins have been forgiven, and our transgressions are not counted against us. Yet we can still choose separation and brokenness by doing the very things we don't want to do. So, becoming whole in shalom requires action on our part to stop falling short in loving well. We are pursuing the continual development of right relationships through growing up in Christ.

When talking about a human' growing up', it is easy to recognise the attributes we correlate to this statement. Babies develop gross and fine motor skills. They learn to talk, and they develop a sense of self. Kids continue to grow physically in height and stature; they grow in their understanding of the world and how it works. Teenagers continue to 'grow up' as they begin maturing in how they apply their understanding of the world and take on more responsibility. But what does it look like as we grow up in Christ? What are the elements we must go through and the attributes of a person who has 'grown up'? These are found throughout the New Testament:

— we work out and see what our salvation established within us (Phil.2:12-13; Eph 1:15-23);

— we set our mind on the Spirit of life and peace (Rom.8:6);

— we seek the things above where Christ is (Col.3:1);

— we put off the old and put on the new (Eph.4:20-24);

— We practise the ways of the Kingdom to defeat the 'muscle memory' of sin in our members (Rom. 7:21-25); and

— we choose to live by design, not by default, to call an end to the vandalism of shalom.

Again, just like children growing into adults, the transition points and pursuits of these things create tension between what I am familiar with and what I am reaching for to become like Jesus. However, tension doesn't mean something is wrong; it means something is happening. In broad terms, what is happening is an invitation to exchange my perspective for His. To understand that God is more interested in my wholeness (character transformation) than in my happiness (the resolution of external circumstances).

Here are some common perspective changes that the Lord will invite you into as you 'grow up' in Christ.

OLD PERSPECTIVE	KINGDOM PERSPECTIVE
Problem	Opportunity
Obligation	Invitation
Performance	Acceptance
Safety and Control	Faith and Obedience
Certainty	Mystery
My achievements	His Majesty
Comparison	Oneness
Earn my Place	Intrinsically worthy
We must agree	Knowing and being Known

The question now is, what perspective will you adopt, and what will you choose to practise?

RIGHTEOUSNESS AND SOUL KEEPING

When we practice, seek, hunger and thirst for righteousness, we are focused on being in right relationship with God, ourselves and others. To become whole in being in right relationship, we need to be attentive to what is shaping and forming our soul.

> *Then Jesus said to His disciples, "If anyone wants to come after Me, he must deny himself, take up his cross, and follow Me. For whoever wants to save his life will lose it; but whoever loses his life for My sake will find it. For what good will it do a person if he gains the whole world, but forfeits his soul? Or what will a person give in exchange for his soul? For the Son of Man is going to come in the glory of His Father with His angels, and will then repay every person according to his deeds.*
>
> Matt. 16:24-27

Genesis 2:7 tells us that God made man a 'living soul'. As a living soul, we are made by God, made for God, and in this context, are made to NEED God. As a living soul, we are needy. We are needy physically, emotionally, psychologically, socially, relationally, economically, and the list goes on. The saying that mankind is infinite in our capacity for desire (neediness) while God is infinite in His capacity to give more (meet needs) has been attributed to Thomas Aquinas.

We live our lives in the tension of being needy and figuring out how to meet those needs. This is why Mark records Jesus as saying:

> *For what does it benefit a person to gain the whole world, and forfeit his soul? For what could a person give in exchange for his soul? For whoever is ashamed of Me and My words in this adulterous and sinful generation, the Son of Man will also be ashamed of him when He comes in the glory of His Father with the holy angels."*
>
> Mark 8:36-38

How we meet our needs has eternal consequences. We can meet our needs based on Jesus' words or based on a self-centred and self-reliant focus that protects us from our fears. We can exchange the well-being of our souls, established in God's ways, for our own ways. We can gain the prestige and comfort of our culture at the expense of right relationships. This can happen because our soul is being formed by self-interest, not the ways of God's Kingdom.

Our physical bodies are formed by what we eat and drink, exercise, our environment, and our emotional well-being. We can choose to be intentional in the influence of these factors, or we can choose to 'live and let live' carelessly. One way or another, our physical bodies will be formed. Similarly, the inner world of our soul is shaped and formed either intentionally or unintentionally.

Our soul integrates, correlates and enlivens everything going on in the various dimensions of our lives. It is our life centre. How do we keep our soul and all its neediness focused on the ways and words of Jesus?

There are many answers to this question to be found in the body of spiritual formation literature. Here I wish to focus on only one.

> *Remember those who led you, who spoke the word of God to you; and considering the result of their way of life, imitate their faith. Jesus Christ is the same yesterday and today, and forever. Do not be misled by varied and strange teachings; for it is good for the heart to be strengthened by grace, not by foods, through which those who were so occupied were not benefited.*
>
> *Through Him then, let's continually offer up a sacrifice of praise to God, that is, the fruit of lips praising His name. And do not neglect doing good and sharing, for with such sacrifices God is pleased. Obey your leaders and submit to them—for they keep watch over your souls as those who will give an account—so that they may do this with joy, not groaning; for this would be unhelpful for you. Pray for us, for we are sure that we have a good conscience, desiring to conduct ourselves honourably in all things.*
>
> Heb. 13:7-9; 15-18

We see here that soul keeping and becoming whole in righteousness must find expression in community. We will all follow others in some way, shape or form. Therefore, consider who you will follow, finding leaders in the community of faith who have successfully gone before you in becoming like Jesus. Then imitate their faith. Learn from them, allowing the history of practices that rely on grace and His empowering presence to guide your formation to becoming more like Jesus.

As we've looked at previously, we will experience reward and loss in eternity based on the choices we make in this life (1 Cor. 3:11-15). A choice that leads to life and reward is choosing to live in community, doing good and sharing with others. A choice to be like Jesus by pursuing a life of humility and serving the needs of others(Phil. 2:5-9). This sets the right environment and context for discovering how to flourish, become whole, and be in right relationships.

Christ-like leadership will be focused on building cultures through values that focus on soul keeping and spiritual formation. They recognise the significance and importance of this to God. Equally, followers recognise the critical role they play in maintaining a culture that regards the place of righteousness highly.

Community is something that doesn't 'just happen' but is built on purpose. In building community, we recognise that the connections we forge with others will enable us to benefit. We benefit from what God is doing in their lives. We give back out of the overflow of our relationship with Jesus to each other. We learn from one another how to live under the direction of a soul surrendered to the ways of Jesus.

Who are you going to choose to do life with?

RELATIONAL FAITHFULNESS AND JOY

Becoming whole in the place of relational faithfulness is helped through knowing how hesed, joy, and brain science come together. Wilder and Hendricks[8] write:

> Perhaps the biggest surprise emerging from brain-scan studies has been that, for our brain, identity develops through attachments. Joyful, secure attachments build a good brain. Fearful or weak attachments build a bad brain. When we say "a bad brain," we mean an identity centre that damages our relationships when we are upset. Character develops through relationships - *hesed* relationships- that can handle times when things go wrong. A secure *hesed* attachment can ride through storms and remain loving. Character in the brain is an expression of an identity that has grown strong and well. As Christians, we want an identity in our brain that looks like Jesus.

Brain scientists have concluded that our brains run on joy like a car runs on fuel, and our brains desire joy more than anything else.[9]

8   Ibid pg 82-83
9   Ibid pg 54

CHAPTER 4

> *You will make known to me the way of life;*
> *In Your presence is fullness of joy;*
> *In Your right hand there are pleasures forever.*
>
> Ps. 16:11
>
> *For You make him most blessed forever;*
> *You make him joyful with the joy of Your presence.*
>
> Ps. 21:6

In both verses, the original language carries the thought that there is joy in God's face. Again, Wilder and Hendricks[10] provide some very helpful thoughts:

> Reading through the Bible and replacing "joy" with the concept of God's face lighting up gives us a better idea of what joy means and how it feels in our bodies. For example, if we rewrite Psalm 16:11 using the fuller definition of joy, "In Your presence is fullness of joy" becomes "When Your face lights up because You are so happy to be
>
> with me, You fill me with joy!" In John 15, Jesus talks about how He loves His disciples with the same love that the Father has for Him. Then He says, "I have told you this so that my joy may be in you and that your joy may be complete" (v.11). If we replace "joy" with the fuller definition, Jesus' statement would be, "My Father's face lights up when He sees Me because I am so special to Him. I'm telling you this so that you will feel how special you are to My Father and to Me. Our faces are shining on you with delight." I can feel that in my body when I picture it. Can you?

With this backdrop, Jesus' words as He prays for us take on a whole new emphasis.

> *But now I am coming to You; and these things I speak in the world so that they may have My joy made full in themselves. I have given them Your word; and the world has hated them because they are not of the world, just as I am not of the world. I am not asking You to take them out of the world, but to keep them away from the evil one. They are not of the world, just as I am not of the world.*
>
> John 17:13-16

---

10 Ibid pg 56-57

Jesus wants us to live with a full measure of His joy. Our joy is made full as we listen to and act on His sayings.

> *These things I have spoken to you so that My joy may be in you, and that your joy may be made full.*

John 15:11

This joy keeps us deeply connected to experiencing His love for us. A love we are to give away to all, including those who hate us. Living in the fullness of His joy and love underpins knowing that we now represent another world. Equally, it positions and equips us to stand in the face of demonic opposition.

> *Consider it all joy, my brothers and sisters, when you encounter various trials, knowing that the testing of your faith produces endurance. And let endurance have its perfect result, so that you may be perfect and complete, lacking in nothing.*

James 1:2-4

> *In this you greatly rejoice, even though now for a little while, if necessary, you have been distressed by various trials, so that the proof of your faith, being more precious than gold which perishes though tested by fire, may be found to result in praise, glory, and honour at the revelation of Jesus Christ; and though you have not seen Him, you love Him, and though you do not see Him now, but believe in Him, you greatly rejoice with joy inexpressible and full of glory, obtaining as the outcome of your faith, the salvation of your souls.*

1 Peter 1:6-9

We are filled with joy as we have spiritual experiences and encounters of God's delight in us; we practise being thankful and expressing gratitude to God; we express, facially and verbally, our delight when we greet and spend time with others; and we pay attention to what causes joy to leak.[11]

What steps could you take to build stronger joyful, secure attachments with others?

WHAT LOVE REQUIRES AND COMMANDMENTS

To become whole in the arena of what love requires necessitates a strong focus on who we are becoming. Paul writes:

---

11 Hendricks, M., & Wilder. J., (2020). *The Other Half of Church*, Moody Publishers, pg .66-69

> *But it is due to Him that you are in Christ Jesus, who became to us wisdom from God, and righteousness and sanctification, and redemption,*
>
> 1 Cor. 1:30

By His doing, we are chosen and called. As we are in Christ, we are forgiven, holy, blameless, and God's beloved. It was wisdom from God to place us in Jesus to experience righteousness, sanctification and redemption. Righteousness: who we have become. Sanctification: who we are becoming. Redemption: who we will become.

God is responsible for our righteousness (right standing) and redemption (a new body). We are responsible for who we are becoming through a commitment to spiritual formation. The only thing we have to offer to God is who we have grown into through our choices. Choices to love with loving devotion and attachment to God. These choices are fuelled by where we abide.

> *Just as the Father has loved Me, I also have loved you; remain in My love. If you keep My commandments, you will remain in My love; just as I have kept My Father's commandments and remain in His love. These things I have spoken to you so that My joy may be in you, and that your joy may be made full.*
>
> John 15:9-11

Keeping Jesus' commandments enables us to remain abiding in loving devotion and attachment. However, what do you hear Jesus saying when He says, "keep My commandments"? Again, as previously noted, the word keep here means to protect; to guard; to watch over. When you hear commandments, do you hear 'the legislated behaviour that is required to remain in right relationship with God'; or an expression of covenant love knowing the choices to be made to serve the interests of God and others?

Legislated behaviour views sin as rebellion against God, leading to a legal or forensic approach to sin. The emphasis is on God's use of regulations to restrain bad behaviour; exercise power over people; and assess us as good or bad. This perspective views abiding as performing appropriately, requiring self-effort, often resulting in guilt, shame, condemnation and fear. Not love!

Expressing covenant love views sin as falling short of expressing love, not falling short of rules and regulations. This approach is based on the truth that we have been included in the family of God (Father, Son, Holy Spirit) as a covenant community of love where our walk with God is relational (not judicial) in nature; we practise and express our new life in Christ by loving others as Jesus loves us. In this, living out the one another's of the New Testament represent the outworking of our spirituality. This perspective views abiding as being accepted; living in grace (the empowering presence of God); and a life of gratitude, reliance and surrender.

Jesus kept His Father's commandments as an expression of covenant love. Jesus abided in love and remained in love by expressing love. We become whole in what love requires in loving attachment and devotion to God's Word, Jesus, the Word in flesh.

> *In the beginning was the Word, and the Word was with God, and the Word was God. He was in the beginning with God. All things came into being through Him, and apart from Him not even one thing came into being that has come into being. In Him was life, and the life was the Light of mankind. And the Light shines in the darkness, and the darkness did not grasp it.*
>
> John 1:1-5

Keeping God's commandments and abiding in His love does not come naturally!

> *I find then the principle that evil is present in me, the one who wants to do good. For I joyfully agree with the law of God in the inner person, but I see a different law in the parts of my body waging war against the law of my mind, and making me a prisoner of the law of sin, the law which is in my body's parts. Wretched man that I am! Who will set me free from the body of this death? Thanks be to God through Jesus Christ our Lord! So then, on the one hand I myself with my mind am serving the law of God, but on the other, with my flesh the law of sin.*
>
> Rom. 7:21-25

Here Paul refers to two different aspects of what it means to be in Christ. Our inner man is the place of our union with Christ. That is because I have been crucified with Christ, I have died with Him, been buried with Him and have risen again with Him (Rom. 6:8-11). Therefore, I am dead to sin as a realm. It is not my nature. I have finished with it, and it has nothing to do with me.

On the other hand, my mortal body, the members of my body, my flesh, still has instincts, propensities, drives and urges. These trigger my brain function so that sin still has power over my body. For example, I use my tongue to defend myself with anger and criticism; I use my sex drive to find gratification and comfort with lust; I yield to my hunger as a place of comfort through overeating. My members have lived under the power of sin and are governed through my neural pathways.

Consequently, to abide in love through keeping the commandments as an expression of covenant community, I need to reprogramme my brain.

> *For the mind set on the flesh is death, but the mind set on the Spirit is life and peace, So then, brothers and sisters, we are under obligation, not to the flesh, to live according to the flesh— for if you are living in accord with the flesh, you are going to die; but if by the Spirit you are putting to death the deeds of the body, you will live. For all who are being led by the Spirit of God, these are sons and daughters of God.*
>
> Rom. 8: 6, 12-14

We follow the Spirit and put to death the deeds of the body when we practise self-awareness and personal responsibility. When life's relationships and circumstances squeeze me, where do I go? How did I get there? We need to see the Word of God as a mirror and not a measure, revealing to us where we are falling short and guiding us towards change. The Word of God is not an instrument of criticism or judgement that results in condemnation, causing withdrawal from the throne of grace in time of need.

TRUST AND SUFFERINGS

One of the greatest paradoxes of following Jesus is that becoming whole in trust is strongly associated with suffering.

Peter saw suffering as normal and encouraged us to find where God is for us in the suffering, and who we can become through the process.

> *After you have suffered for a little while, the God of all grace, who called you to His eternal glory in Christ, will Himself perfect, confirm, strengthen and establish you.*
>
> 1 Peter 5:10

Jesus declared that it is inevitable that we will have tribulation in life: inner turmoil of confusion, disappointment, discouragement, being irritable, feeling disempowered, being lonely and more. However, He called us to find Him and who He wants to be for us in these times.

> *"These things I have spoken to you, so that in Me you may have peace. In the world you have tribulation, but take courage: I have overcome the world."*

John 16:33

In pastoring the church in Rome, Paul had revelation that tribulation, inner turmoil, was inevitable, and he provided wisdom on how to navigate our way around the pain.

> *And not only this, but we exult in our tribulations, knowing that tribulation brings about perseverance; and perseverance, proven character; and proven character, hope; and hope does not disappoint, because the love of God has been poured out within our hearts through the Holy Spirit who was given to us.*

Rom. 5:3-5

Peter, Jesus and Paul are all 'normalising' pain. Pain is inevitable, but how do we navigate through our pain and find meaning in it? For all three, their navigational aid is having the right posture or stance in the circumstances. The posture they all point to can be captured in one word. Hope.

Hope is a confident expectation of good. We often define good as something being resolved; having certainty; being in control; the circumstances making sense. However, Kingdom expressions of hope are earthed in a deeper relationship with God, myself and others where experiences of love, experiences of servanthood and the development of humility increase and grow in me.

These deeper relationships are built on and through trust. Suffering places a demand on trust, we have to grow and increase in capacity. Paul understood this when he writes:

> *What then shall we say to these things? If God is for us, who is against us? He who did not spare His own Son, but delivered Him over for us all, how will He not also with Him freely give us all things?*

Rom. 8:31-32

The 'things' (verse 31) Paul is encouraging us to speak to are sufferings and weaknesses:

> *For I consider that the sufferings of this present time are not worthy to be compared with the glory that is to be revealed to us.*

Rom.8:18

Now in the same way the Spirit also helps our weakness; for we do not know what to pray for as we should, but the Spirit Himself intercedes for us with groanings too deep for words;

Rom.8:26

We are to respond to sufferings and weaknesses by choosing to place our trust in who God is for us and what He is prepared to give us.

CONCLUSION

Becoming whole through transformation and spiritual formation so as not to contribute to the chaos of relationships is a lifelong pursuit. This pursuit will often occur in challenging circumstances. In these moments, we are to focus first on who we are becoming before what we should do. They are opportunities to determine our future through what we practise before sorting out the present. The posture we take in these times is one where we focus on the prize of our life with God flourishing, not the price of any circumstantial torment being experienced.

This pursuit recognises there is a battle over how I establish a sense of well-being and how I define myself. It requires: the removal and displacement of any idols I rely on to maintain a sense of well-being and certainty of identity; a lifestyle of humility and surrender in embracing who Jesus is for me and in me; belief that my well-being and identity are secured in His Lordship and acceptance of me, not in what I or others have decided is required and necessary.

If I was with you face to face, I would illustrate these ideas like this: I would hold up an unopened, full plastic bottle of water. As I held it, I'd attempt to bring all my strength to bear on it and to crush it. However, I would have no success because the internal pressure is greater than the external pressure I can exert.

I'd then remove the lid, drink some of the contents, replace the lid and again exert external pressure with my hand. The plastic bottle begins to be crushed as the internal pressure is not strong enough to withstand the external force.

When life squeezes you through negative actions and activity, do you find yourself being 'crushed' somehow, or is the internal strength & pressure strong enough to withstand the external? This is what Jesus was pointing to when He said, "You will all be scattered, yet I will not be alone".

Jesus replied to them, "Do you now believe? Behold, an hour is coming, and has already come, for you to be scattered, each to his own home, and to leave Me alone; and yet I am not alone, because the Father is with Me. These things I have spoken to you so that in Me you may have peace. In the world you have tribulation, but take courage; I have overcome the world."

John 16:31-33

Jesus had an understanding that His inner man was stronger and more robust than His circumstances. This is the gift He has for us that He wants us to live from. Paul prayed that the eyes of our heart would be opened:

For this reason I too, having heard of the faith in the Lord Jesus which exists among you and your love for all the saints, do not cease giving thanks for you, while making mention of you in my prayers; that the God of our Lord Jesus Christ, the Father of glory, may give you a spirit of wisdom and of revelation in the knowledge of Him. I pray that the eyes of your heart may be enlightened, so that you will know what is the hope of His calling, what are the riches of the glory of His inheritance in the saints, and what is the boundless greatness of His power toward us who believe. These are in accordance with the working of the strength of His might which He brought about in Christ, when He raised Him from the dead and seated Him at His right hand in the heavenly places, far above all rule and authority and power and dominion, and every name that is named, not only in this age but also in the one to come. And He put all things in subjection under His feet, and made Him head over all things to the church, which is His body, the fullness of Him who fills all in all.

Eph. 1:15-23

He desired that we would walk in a manner worthy of our calling. A calling to oneness with God and to being one with one another. To be diligent in preserving the unity and the bonds of peace by healing our own brokenness that contributes to creating chaos in relationships. I have heard it said that the same boiling water that softens potatoes causes an egg to be hard boiled. We can't blame our circumstances.

CHAPTER 4

SUMMARY

- Living in oneness with one another is a sacred duty.
- To abide in love, the first value to hold is shalom.
- Shalom speaks of reconciliation, yet we live with separation.
- To abide in love, the second value to hold is righteousness.
- We are to practise righteousness in pursuing right relationships.
- To abide in love, the third value to hold is relational faithfulness.
- Our shared love, not our shared interests, holds us together.
- To abide in love, the fourth value to hold is to discover what love requires.
- For love to flourish, it is necessary to protect loving God's way as our most precious approach to life.
- To abide in love, the fifth value to hold to is trust.
- We are to trust God with our purpose, identity, relationships and lives because He loves us just as He loves Jesus.
- Our brokenness undermines our sacred duty to live in oneness with others.
- To become whole in the value of shalom, we need to change our perspective for His.
- To become whole in the value of righteousness, we need to be attentive to what is shaping and forming our soul.
- To become whole in the place of relational faithfulness, we need to know how hesed, joy and brain science come together.
- To become whole in the arena of what love requires necessitates a strong focus on who we are becoming.
- To become whole in how we trust requires the capacity to grow while suffering.

QUESTIONS AND ACTIVITIES

1. Identify how you have historically responded to challenges in relationships that have resulted in you not fulfilling your sacred duty to live in oneness.

2. What could you practise to become more whole in the areas where your ways have undermined your sacred duty?

3. Which of the five values we hold to abide in love is your strongest? How did you become strong in adhering to this value?

4. Which of the five values we hold in order to abide in love is your weakest? What is the Holy Spirit showing you to help you strengthen this value?

Chapter 5

A Call to Action

...Principles and Values that Activate Oneness with One Another

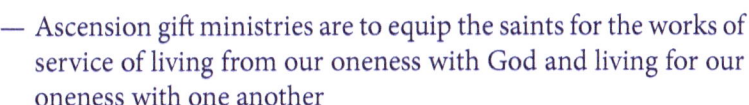

— Ascension gift ministries are to equip the saints for the works of service of living from our oneness with God and living for our oneness with one another

— Leaders contribute to the development of Kingdom cultures when they embody Kingdom culture and love

— Embodiment requires behaviour that: builds trust; prioritises being a learning community; and that never sacrifices strength of relationship for achievement

— Leaders equip others for oneness with one another when they have values and practices that celebrate transformation in their personal spiritual formation

— There is a profound difference between leader development and leadership development

— It is the sacred duty of apprentices of Jesus to only offer personal opinions that give value, particularly where there is tension.

Jesus said He would build His church. He asked us to build people, that is, make disciples. However, church history, both old and new, is full of examples where man has taken on the role of building the church, not disciples.

This misplacement of roles was particularly evident in the late eight and early nine hundreds in the Catholic church. At that time, the papacy was marred by corruption and greed and was dominated by Rome's powerful families and the German kings. Being the pope was seen as a prize and powerful men committed all kinds of atrocities to achieve that position. Over a ninety-three year period between 872 and 965, there was a total of twenty-four popes. However, extraordinarily, between 896 and 904, there was a new pope every year! Thirty-three per cent of the total number of popes over 93 years held office in eight-point six per cent of the time frame![1]

One of the more bizarre moments in church history took place during this time. An extraordinary example of how a man wanted to build the church rather than build people.

> The Cadaver Synod took place in January 897 in the Church of St. John Lateran (Basilica di San Giovanni in Laterano), which is the pope's official seat in his role as the Bishop of Rome. It happened after the current pontiff, Stephen VII, was incentivised to hold this trial by a powerful Roman family who had been extremely politically against Fomosus, the former pope. Formosus (Latin for "good looking") had been an elderly pope who had died on April 4, 896.
>
> Stephen presided over this trial himself, appointing members of the Roman clergy as co-judges. In order for the accused to appear in the trial, they disentombed him from his grave in St. Peter's Basilica, dressed the rotting corpse in pontifical vestments, and set him up in a chair. Behind the chair, they ordered a young deacon to defend Formosus by speaking for him.
>
> The charges were read. Formosus stood, accused of perjury, coveting the papacy and violating church canons when he was elected pope (Wilkes Jr., 2001). Stephen VII conducted the whole trial as the remaining clergy watched in horror. He screamed, insulted, and mocked the decaying corpse of his predecessor as if he were

---

[1] I was raised a catholic. At the age of 8 I wanted to be a priest. In the last 25 years I have met many lovers of Jesus who practise their faith in the Catholic church. I have the pleasure and privilege of mentoring a young catholic priest. I have great respect and love for their people. It's important to note that and that in these comments, I am not providing commentary on the Catholic church, but simply stating historically accurate facts.

alive. The young deacon would occasionally defend his dead charge by weakly proclaiming his innocence. Still, Formosus ended up being convicted as guilty on all charges.

After declaring Formosus as guilty, Stephen set his sentence. Three of his fingers from his right hand, the ones used for papal blessings, were taken off. All of the acts and ordinances (that is consecrations, appointments and ordinations) from Formosus' reign were invalidated. Finally, the already decaying body was stripped of his papal vestments, dressed in the clothes of a layperson and buried in a common grave.[2]

While this story and example is extreme, it plays out more subtly in church communities still today. Paul speaks to the change in us as we mature in Christ, moving from the trickery of people and craftiness in deceitful scheming to speaking the truth in love and growing up in all aspects into Him who is the head, that is Christ.

> *And He gave some as apostles, some as prophets, some as evangelists, some as pastors and teachers, for the equipping of the saints for the work of ministry, for the building up of the body of Christ; until we all attain to the unity of the faith, and of the knowledge of the Son of God, to a mature man, to the measure of the stature which belongs to the fullness of Christ. As a result, we are no longer to be children, tossed here and there by waves and carried about by every wind of doctrine, by the trickery of people, by craftiness in deceitful scheming; but speaking the truth in love, we are to grow up in all aspects into Him who is the head, that is, Christ, from whom the whole body, being fitted and held together by what every joint supplies, according to the proper working of each individual part, causes the growth of the body for the building up of itself in love.*
>
> Eph.4:11-16

These familiar verses are shared in the context of Paul addressing our oneness with God (Eph 1:1-2:10), our oneness with one another (Eph. 2:11-22; 4:1-6), and providing two reasons for the pursuit of oneness with one another (Eph.3:1-21). Seeing these verses in context warrants the exploration of the thought that the role of apostles, prophets, evangelists, pastors and teachers (that is, leaders) is to equip the saints to live in oneness with God and oneness with one another - the works of service.

---

[2] History of Yesterday, (n.d), The Haunting Tale of the Cadaver Synod, Retrieved 3rd September 2021 from https://historyofyesterday.com/the-trial-of-the-dead-pop-bbfbbf60e292

Ephesians 4:11-16 calls leaders with ascension gift ministries to equip the saints for the work of service. The ideas that follow this call in Ephesians 4:17 to 6:24 are ALL related to living from our oneness with God and for our oneness with one another.

To draw it out more specifically, Paul speaks to <u>living from our oneness with God</u> in verses 13 and 15 of chapter 4:

- the knowledge of the Son of God, to a mature man, to the measure of the stature that belongs to the fullness of Christ

- we are to grow up in all aspects into Him who is the head, even Christ.

He then speaks to <u>living for our oneness with one another</u> in verses 12, 13, 15 and 16:

- to the building up of the body of Christ;

- until we all attain to the unity of the faith;

- but speaking the truth in love;

- and, from whom the whole body, being fitted and held together by what every joint supplies, according to the proper working of each individual part, causes the growth of the body for the building up of itself in love.

If we fail to pay attention to our transformation as leaders, living from oneness with God and for oneness with each other, we revert to living by default and not by design. This has an impact on the organisations and people we lead, identified by Bolsinger[3] like this:

> Leadership is focused on what can be or what must be.... leadership is about an organisation fulfilling its mission and realising its reason for being.... leadership is always about corporate and personal transformation.... if someone is not functioning as a leader, the system will always default to the status quo.

We see the impact of this default on the status quo in the western church, evidenced by the significant decline in people identifying as part of the local church. The traditional church has been focused on maintaining Christian culture, creed and faith practices to ensure its existence in the future, all while continuing to decline. The rise of individualism and consumerism has seen

---

3   Bolsinger. T., (2018). Canoeing the Mountains. IVP Books, Illinois, pg 21

more progressive churches responding by positioning themselves as another option for those seeking personal fulfilment. Social media, as a forum for all opinions, has accelerated a culture of judgement and criticism. In defence of creeds, 'my' doctrine and 'true' Christian practices, Christians have adopted positions of judgement and criticism.

While it can be tempting to 'stick with what we know' and do more of the same because it feels safe and familiar, Holy Spirit is inviting Christian leaders to rediscover the place of corporate and personal transformation. He is drawing us to focus on the truth that God has a church to fulfil His mission in the world. A mission that requires we fully embrace becoming one with God and one with one another. That we become a church that lives by principles and values leading to the representation of God's Kingdom, not the kingdoms of this world.

PRINCIPLES AND VALUES THAT MAKE ONENESS A PRIORITY

Bolsinger[4] helps us understand the interaction between culture, values and behaviours when he writes:

> Culture is the combination of actual values and concrete actions that shape the warp and woof of organisational life… the actual behaviours of those in authority express and shape the actual values of the organisational culture.

Leaders contribute to the development of Kingdom cultures when they embody Kingdom culture and love. This creates a healthy environment for shared values to guide all decision making that results in oneness with one another. The leaders' primary pursuit is the development and maintenance of healthy relationships before but not without answers, progress and fruitful results. This is achieved by creating non-negotiable approaches to conflict where heightened emotions encounter questions for which there are no easy answers.

'Great thought', I can hear you say, but how? I'd like to suggest that there are three key behaviours (principles) that create actual values for pursuing a life together that results in living in oneness with one another. It is important to note that while the role of the leader is critical in setting culture, the role of those who join their team also plays a critical role in supporting that set culture. Any team member who doesn't equally own these three key behaviours will inevitably create division and chaos. The following key behaviours must be owned and pursued by all.

---

4   Ibid pg 74

The first behaviour is trust. Stephen Covey[5] captures the imperative nature of trust well when he writes:

> There is one thing that is common to every individual, relationship, team, family, organisation, nation, economy, and civilisation throughout the world – one thing which, if removed, will destroy the most powerful government, the most successful business, the most thriving economy, the greatest friendship, the strongest character, the deepest love.
>
> … That one thing is trust.
>
> Trust impacts us 24/7, 365 days a year. It undergirds and affects the quality of every relationship, every communication, every work project, every business venture, every effort in which we are engaged. It changes the quality of every present moment and alters the trajectory and outcome of every future moment of our lives – both personally and professionally.
>
> … I contend that the ability to establish, grow, extend and restore trust is not only vital to our personal and interpersonal well-being; it is *the* key leadership competency of the new global economy.
>
> I am also convinced that in every situation, nothing is as fast as the speed of trust. And, contrary to popular belief, trust is something you *can* do something about. In fact, you can get good at creating it!

This theme is constant in leadership literature. Trust is the irreducible minimum in leadership. Trust is something that we can and must build through consistent actions. Actions that are the expression of our character and values. Trust comes from the congruence of leaders repeatedly doing what they say. Bolsinger[6] says it this way:

> Relational congruence is the ability to be fundamentally the same person with the same values in every relationship, in every circumstance and especially amidst every crisis. It is the internal capacity to keep promises to God, to self and to one's relationships that consistently express one's identity and values in spiritually and emotionally healthy ways. Relational congruence is about both *constancy* and *care* at the same time. It is about both character and affection, and self-knowledge and authentic self-expression. Rela-

---

5 Covey, Stephen M.R., (2006). The Speed of Trust, Free Press, USA, pg 1-2
6 Bolsinger. T., op. cit. pg 67-68

tional congruence is the leader's ability to cultivate strong, healthy, caring relationships, maintain healthy boundaries, and communicate clear expectations, all while staying focused on the mission.

This type of congruence is established as we design our lives around a commitment to integrity, continually growing in and acting out of our maturity, protecting and enhancing our emotional health and living with authenticity in all our relationships.

The second behaviour required for a culture where oneness is a priority is being a learning community. In this context, Bolsinger[7] provides further insight:

> The key to surviving in a world filled with unknowns is keeping a constant posture of curiosity, awareness and attention.... we are not normally inclined towards these characteristics.

There are many enemies that will try and stand in the way of developing a culture of oneness with one another. Anxiety, relational tension, bitterness, anger, resentment, judgement, criticism and fighting for a cause to name a few. Becoming a learning community that values conversations of discovery above prosecution will help stand against these enemies. A learning community looks like people who are motivated to understand another's point of view, perspective, or position. They have a higher value for knowing and loving those around them than changing them. They seek the middle ground where there's a sharing of common understanding. Tensions are not resolved by establishing right or wrong. Tension results in the pursuit of self-awareness and personal responsibility to discover what is happening in me and for others.

Oneness with others will not be achieved where there are good guys and bad guys. Nor will it be achieved where the motivation is to be right, punish others, or find a scapegoat. These positions shut down a desire to learn, hear, and discover. They promote an approach that wants to prosecute a case from a closed knowledge set, having already arrived at conclusions.

Learning communities do not live with a 'fix it' mentality. Instead, they journey together in a process to find and develop new beliefs and values of being in oneness with one another. To travel this road well, it's important that we value observations, interpretations and interventions.

Observations from the people around us are important because we all know and see only in part. All observations need to be heard and considered. This

---

7   Ibid pg 108

isn't always easy as your emotional buttons are being pushed. However, adopting a posture of humility and teachability is critical to enable the honest consideration, but not necessarily acceptance, of all observations.

Interpretations of an event or situation invariably reflect what a person values. When we need to fight to protect our oneness, competing values are often being presented, which can be difficult to navigate as each is valuable. Maintaining the value of each interpretation when some will not prevail creates tension, leading to being stuck. For individuals creating or supporting the culture, surrender becomes a key value here. Surrender, in this instance, is the ability to sacrifice your point of view to serve the broader perspective.

Sometimes, as we learn and discover together, interventions are required. Interventions in this context are where a person, generally the leader, needs to step in and make some decisions for the benefit of the whole. In a loving community, interventions are not seen as the end of the process. Instead, they are the next step in learning as together observations are made about the impact of the intervention. Often, but not always, interventions can involve loss and change, which can be big 'trigger points' for many people. In a learning community, there is a commitment from all members to strengthening relationships regardless of the functional outcome of the situation.

The third behaviour to make oneness with one another the highest priority is to never sacrifice strength of relationship for achievement. It is important to stay focused on what needs to get done. When conflict or change is being pursued, Bolsinger[8] suggests the following approach:

> Start with conviction,
>
> stay calm,
>
> stay connected, and
>
> stay the course.
>
> Staying calm acknowledges that environments of conflict and change can be heated and testy. The heat generally comes from urgency and/or anxiety. How the leader responds emotionally to the urgency and/or anxiety is vital. The calm leader is self-aware enough to find places of self-control, kindness and patience in their responses. This is their highest priority while still being courageous enough to keep the process moving toward a fruitful outcome.

---
8   Ibid pg 128

> Equally, the prevailing organisational culture needs to share values that call on everyone involved to be aware of their responses so that the anxiety and or anger of others does not derail relational well-being and equity. We are all called to regulate ourselves. For the leaders though, to lead means to have some command of our own anxiety and capacity not to let other people's anxiety contaminate us; that is, not to allow their anxiety to affect our thinking, actions and decisions.[9]

The actual behaviours of trust, being a learning community and making oneness with one another the highest priority are facilitated by digging wells, not building fences. That is, creating environments that attract people to explore and discover the wonder of being one with God and others while avoiding the establishment of rules and behaviour that define what is needed for acceptance. It is an environment and culture where love restores that which is broken.

> *Brothers **and sisters**, even if a person is caught in any wrongdoing, you who are spiritual are to restore such a person in a spirit of gentleness; **each one** looking to yourself, so that you are not tempted as well. Bear one another's burdens, and thereby fulfil the law of Christ.*
>
> Galatians 6:1-2

PRINCIPLES AND VALUES THAT CREATE A CULTURE THAT CELEBRATES TRANSFORMATION

Paul identifies that leaders equip the saints to live in oneness with God and one another. This equipping occurs as leaders create a culture that prioritises values and behaviours, leading to a life rooted in our oneness with God and characterised by practices that lead to oneness with others.

In Ephesians 4:17-24, Paul revisits his explorations of the place of living a life that practises transformation.

> *But you did not learn Christ in this way, if indeed you have heard Him and have been taught in Him, just as truth is in Jesus, that, in reference to your former way of life, you are to rid yourselves of the old self, which is being corrupted in accordance with the lusts of deceit, and that you are to be renewed in the spirit of your minds, and to put on the new self, which in the likeness of God has been created in righteousness and holiness of the truth.*

---

9   Ibid pg 148

To embed the value and significance of transformation in spiritual formation in a culture requires leaders to have values and practices that celebrate transformation. Transformation being defined by *who we are becoming* before, but not without, activity and outcomes.

The story of Mary and Martha is illustrative of this value (Luke 10:38-42). Jesus did not criticise Martha's activity. Rather, he pointed to some lessons in maintaining oneness. First, Jesus highlighted that activity has the power to create worry and anxiety. Second, Jesus prioritises the necessity of listening to and receiving from Jesus over activity and outcomes. He does not dismiss or criticise the place of activity and outcomes. Rather, He highlights that our listening and receiving in our various roles facilitate opportunities for transformation. Again, self-awareness and personal responsibility are imperative to hear and see where we have inner turmoil and respond as Holy Spirit invites us to wholeness in those areas.

Brene Brown[10] provides excellent insights into identifying values and behaviour that facilitate the development of a culture that celebrates transformation. One of the critical elements of transformation is courage, the willingness to face areas of lack or pain that need restoration.

As Brown explores the values and behaviours that cultivate a culture where transformation is celebrated, she first identifies that you can't get to courage without rumbling and vulnerability.

> A rumble is a discussion, conversation, or meeting defined by a commitment to lean into vulnerability, to stay curious and generous, to stick with the messy middle of problem identification and solving, to take a break and circle back when necessary, to be fearless in owning our own parts, and, as psychologist Harriet Lerner teaches, to listen with the same passion with which we want to be heard. More than anything else, when someone says, "Let's rumble," it cues me to show up with an open heart and mind so we can serve the work and each other, not our egos.

It is important to note that vulnerability includes 'listening with the same passion with which we want to be heard'. It is not simply transparency that lays out your stuff on the table. Instead, it is a position that says, 'here is my stuff; I'm going to allow you to speak to it'.

Brown goes on to explore and establish shared language, skills, tools and daily practices that support us in these conversations. These practices are a re-

---

10   Brown, B., (2018). Dare to Lead, Penguin Random House Publishing, London, pg 10-15

sponse to discovering where we need to put off the old and put on the new. In Brown's language, the four key skill sets are:

- Rumbling with Vulnerability;
- Leaning into our Values;
- Braving Trust; and
- Learning to Rise.

If we take this language and put it into the context of pursuing oneness with God and one another, we could say the practices required are:

- embracing our vulnerabilities, allowing God and others to speak into areas where we might be missing something;
- being integrous in the application of Kingdom values;
- discovering how to build bridges of trust (and not blow them up); and,
- learning how to grow up in who we are in Christ.

Secondly, Brown identifies that behaviours of self-awareness and self-love matter when creating a culture that celebrates transformation because who we are is how we live and lead. Brown notes that this self-awareness and self-love are particularly important when it comes to fear, the emotion that is so often at the centre of problematic behaviours and culture. It isn't so much whether we feel it or not; rather, the importance is in how we respond to our fear when we are aware of feeling it.

Thirdly, Brown identifies that a culture that celebrates transformation is one that expects people to be in pursuit of a whole heart (i.e. It presupposes that we will make mistakes and have areas that require growth and attention). That 'armouring up' to win (going to self-protection mode) is not necessary nor rewarded. It is a culture that has practices vigilantly held to where people are safe, seen, heard and respected.

Through research-based evidence, Brown identifies that a leader's care for and connection to others are the irreducible requirements for developing a culture that celebrates transformation.

There is a profound difference between leader development and leadership development. Leader development focuses on character and transformation.

Leadership development focuses on skill and achieving outcomes. Both are required. However, one is to be prioritised to support values and practices that develop a culture where transformation is celebrated.

Peter Scazzero's[11] seminal book speaks powerfully to this reality:

> Who you are is more important than what you do. Why? Because the love of Jesus in you is the greatest gift you have to give to others. Mature spiritual leadership is forged in the crucible of difficult conversations, the pressure of conflicted relationships, the pain of setbacks, and dark nights of the soul. Out of these experiences, we come to understand the complex nature of our inner world. Moreover, as we develop new practices and rhythms robust enough to withstand the pressures that leadership exerts on the inner life, we naturally become stronger and more effective leaders. And we move on from simply affirming truth and wisdom to owning and applying what we know.

There is the old adage that more is caught than taught in life. Jesus made disciples by inviting them into His life to see first-hand how He lived. He invited them to imitate Him. Paul offered the same invitation (1 Corinthians 11:1). A culture that celebrates transformation is established by leaders who illustrate the ways of transformation and a life of spiritual formation openly. Like Mary, they prioritise an apprenticeship to Jesus based in a life of listening, learning and receiving. Where their becoming informs their doing, they find how to be like Jesus in the controversies, tensions and discouragement that life brings. In so doing, they live a life of discovery that others can follow. A culture emerges where everyone can reach for completeness, flourishing and maturity.

> *You have heard it said, 'You shall love your neighbour and hate your enemy.' But I say to you, love your enemies and pray for those who persecute you, so that you may prove yourselves to be sons of your Father who is in heaven; for He causes His sun to rise on the evil and the good, and sends rain on the righteous and the unrighteous. For if you love those who love you, what reward do you have? Even the tax collectors, do they not do the same? And if you greet only your brothers and sisters, what more are you doing than others? Even the Gentiles, do they not do the same? Therefore, you shall be perfect, as your heavenly Father is perfect.*
>
> Matthew 5:43-48

---

11 Scazzero. P., (2015). The Emotionally Healthy Leader, Zondervan, Michigan Illinois, pg 38, 50

CHAPTER 5

PRINCIPLES AND VALUES THAT CREATE A CULTURE OF ONENESS

We've explored how leaders must establish and model the values and practices required to develop a culture that celebrates transformation and where oneness with one another is a priority. However, all of God's people have a sacred duty to pursue oneness with one another.

Ephesians 4:25-6:18 describes practices to be pursued so oneness with one another is prioritised and transformation celebrated and the outcomes when we do these things. Paul asserts that we need to act on what needs to be laid aside (4:25); that we should be imitators of God (5:1); be careful who we partner with (5:7), and be careful how we walk (5:15). The outcomes of these behaviours include oneness in marriage (5:22-23), oneness in family life (6:1-9), and awareness of the place of spiritual warfare in undermining oneness with one another (6:10-18).

The fulcrum and centrepiece to these things being accomplished is:

> *and subject yourselves to one another in the fear of Christ.*
>
> Eph. 5:21

It is our sacred duty to live in submission to one another. If we hold a heartfelt reverence for Jesus and who we are in Him, it will be evidenced by how we choose to be subject to one another. To honour all other people is to honour Jesus.

Jesus prayed that this would be the value and behaviour we bring to all our relationships.

> *The glory which You have given Me I also have given to them, so that they may be one, just as We are one; I in them and You in Me, that they may be perfected in unity, so that the world may know that You sent Me, and You loved them, just as You loved Me.*
>
> John 17:22-23

As noted previously, the word glory here from the original language means 'to offer a personal opinion that gives value'. The Father only ever offers personal opinions of Jesus that give Jesus value. Jesus, in turn, only ever offers personal opinions of us that give us value. Jesus identifies that this is the key to living in oneness with others.

Our sacred duty as apprentices to Jesus is to only give personal opinions that give others value. However, our fears, insecurities, lack of emotional health, and wholeness contribute to our being self-centred and self-reliant. While we are pursuing a lifestyle of transformation, our brokenness will inevitably contribute to tension in relationships. Relational tension emerges across life regularly and threatens love and oneness. Differences of opinion and natural tendencies will often draw this out. For example, a difference in political persuasion, left or right; differences in communication styles; opinions on the use of financial resources; differences in risk appetites - high or low; different shopping styles (are you a hunter or gatherer); theological differences; church life practices; leadership styles; recreational preferences; how to raise children; another's driving abilities; where to squeeze the toothpaste tube from; and, the list goes on!

When we are faced with tension in relationships, we have a choice. An 'old man' response leads to us choosing criticism or judgement of others, which undermines our willingness and capacity to offer personal opinions that give value.

A new man response, one that prioritises oneness and love, must recognise and understand that in most instances where relational tension is present that: TENSION DOESN'T MEAN SOMETHING IS WRONG; IT MEANS SOMETHING IS HAPPENING.

What does it look like to recognise that something is happening but not wrong?

WHEN SOMETHING IS WRONG	WHEN SOMETHING IS HAPPENING
Communicate to be proven right	Communicate to know and be known
Prosecute a case or cause	Discover all perspectives and sides
Ascribe intent and motive	Ask questions before coming to conclusions
Justice(fairness) becomes the thermometer	Understanding becomes the barometer
Judgement prevails	Mercy is given
Behaviour is defensive and justifying	Considerate and enquiring
Blame is attributed	Self-awareness and personal responsibility are enacted
Use of authority for conformity is relied upon	Accountability for transformation is leaned into
Fear, insecurity, and identity issues prevail	Knowledge of being loved, secure, and accepted while growing
Prejudice is ascribed	Compassion is given
Critical and condemning remarks are made	Commentary and observation are offered
A posture of offence is taken	A posture of forgiveness is adopted
Resolution needed for control	Patience is pursued to bring perspective

CHAPTER 5

When we lean into a posture that says, 'something is wrong', the true condition of our heart is revealed. The most common condition revealed is a dual standard, a desire that I receive mercy and everyone else receives justice. This condition is powerfully illustrated in the story of blind Bartimaeus.

> *Then they came to Jericho. And later, as He was leaving Jericho with His disciples and a large crowd, a beggar who was blind named Bartimaeus, the son of Timaeus, was sitting by the road. And when he heard that it was Jesus the Nazarene, he began to cry out and say, "Jesus, Son of David, have mercy on me!" Many were sternly telling him to be quiet, but he kept crying out all the more, "Son of David, have mercy on me!" And Jesus stopped and said, "Call him here." So they called the man who was blind, saying to him, "Take courage, stand up! He is calling for you." And throwing off his cloak, he jumped up and came to Jesus. And replying to him, Jesus said, "What do you want Me to do for you?" And the man who was blind said to Him, "Rabboni, I want to regain my sight!" And Jesus said to him, "Go; your faith has made you well." And immediately he regained his sight and began following Him on the road.*

Mark 10:46-52

Here, Bartimaeus is seeking mercy. Those following Jesus, His disciples included, were being 'stern' in wanting to keep him away from Jesus. Culturally, his blindness would have been judged to be a consequence of sin.

> *And His disciples asked Him, "Rabbi, who sinned, this man or his parents, that he would be born blind?"*

John 9:2

Consequently, the disciples and the crowd following deemed that Bartimaeus had to live under the penalty of justice. It is difficult to know what was motivating those that called, saying, "Take courage, stand up! He is calling you." However, the tone from them seems to be one of 'be careful'. It appears that those speaking didn't volunteer to help Bartimaeus to stand up. They left him to make his own way. Even when Jesus called, those who had tried to keep Bartimaeus away were still not convinced Jesus would respond kindly to the request for mercy.

The question to explore here is: what leads us to pursue justice for everyone else yet mercy for ourselves? I have previously explored our attraction to and propensity towards judgement. We have been seduced by the father of lies to locate value and worth in performance, not acceptance. The cultural influences of family, ethnic background, socioeconomic status and religion have combined to give us the illusion that we have the right to decide what is right. We have been conditioned to conclude what is appropriate and required based on expectations. Add to these realities our own brokenness displayed through fear, shame, and control, then justice (the retributive kind, not the restorative kind!) becomes the focal point. Justice becomes the goal.

Another contributing factor is the pursuit of life rhythms focused on fruitfulness, accomplishment, organisation and strategy. These rhythms invariably override the value we place on relationships framed through knowing and being known, discovery, honour; respect; and mutual submission. We lose sight of our sacred duty to be subject to one another in the fear of Christ. Instead, we choose to live through self-reliance and self-centeredness that calls us to resolve tension through 'our truth' based on our justice.

Conversely, leaning into a posture that says, 'something is happening' reveals a heart that seeks self-awareness and takes personal responsibility. It embraces a life of spiritual transformation. It celebrates the opportunity as an apprentice of Jesus to grow up into His life, way and values. This posture empowers our sacred duty to be faithful in relationships, to be in right relationship, and, to be diligent to pursue oneness with others.

SUMMARY

— The role of apostles, prophets, evangelists, pastors and teachers is to equip the saints to live in oneness with God and others.

— The Holy Spirit is inviting Christian leaders to rediscover that God has a church for HIS mission in the world. A mission that fully embraces becoming one with God and with one another.

— Leaders contribute to Kingdom culture being developed through their clarity, embodiment of Kingdom principles, and love.

— Living in oneness with others requires values and behaviours of trust, being a learning community, and making oneness with one another the highest priority.

— Learning communities value conversations of discovery over prosecution.

- To discover how to live in oneness with one another requires values and behaviour that celebrate spiritual formation and personal transformation.

- We are to pursue a life focused on who we are becoming before but not without a life focused on activity and outcomes.

- All of God's people have a sacred duty to pursue oneness with one another.

- Tension doesn't mean something is wrong; it means something is happening.

QUESTIONS AND ACTIVITY

1. What non-negotiable values are you prepared to live from that would empower you to resolve conflict and tension with the goal of remaining in right relationship with others?

2. How would you transition from a 'fix it' mentality based in prosecuting your case to a 'learning' mentality based in discovery so that your relationships can be strengthened?

3. What could you do to grow in your commitment and pursuit of self-awareness and personal responsibility as the cornerstone of your transformation to be like Jesus?

4. If you believe who you are is more important than what you do, what three aspects of your inner world would the Holy Spirit want you to strengthen to empower you to love and remain in right relationship with others?

Concluding Words

STAY THE COURSE

— … that they may all be one; just as You, Father, are in Me and I in you, that they also may be in Us, so that the world may believe You sent Me.

John 17:21

As I wrap up part two in this four-part journey of discovering what it looks like to be Radically Restored to Oneness, I wanted to close with an encouragement.

I've been pastoring for coming up to 40 years. Before that, I was a social worker working with some of the worst child abuse cases in New South Wales, Australia. I have seen the drastic and damaging impacts that living with a framework of judgement, a lack of willingness to own your own stuff (self-awareness and personal responsibility) and a drive for justice at all costs can have. It is not pretty.

I have also been privileged to be part of relationships and communities that pursue living out oneness with one another. It is beautiful, wonderful, rich, rewarding and awe-inspiring. Conflict becomes fertile soil for love to abound and growth to occur. Relationships like this pull you in and draw you close, even when you're at your worst. It is a stunning gift.

Having walked this journey of pursuing oneness for several years now, although I will be the first to admit, imperfectly, I know there will be days when it all feels too hard, not fair and that it would be easier to revert to the old familiar ways. I know this without a doubt because I have been there too! This is not an easy road.

I want to encourage you, though, when it feels hard to stay committed to living in oneness with one another, stay the course!! Keep your eyes on Jesus, the author and perfector of your faith. Not only will it benefit you as you become more like Him, look more like Love and live a rich life, sometimes (often!) in the midst of chaos, it will start to rub off. Perhaps you will give those around you a window into what a life fully surrendered to the way of Jesus looks like, and they will want to live like that too.

Remember what we have learned:

— We are called to practice our spirituality in community; indeed, it cannot be fully formed anywhere else

— The Kingdom of God is relational and has relational values

— We need to practice diligently activity that creates oneness with others; it doesn't just happen

— We need to be transformed as we abide in Love

— And we need to activate oneness through the culture we create.

As we live this out, we will become the answer to Jesus' prayer

> *"... that they may all be one; just as You, Father, are in Me and I in you, that they also may be in Us, so that the world may believe You sent Me."*

John 17:21

And what a wonderful thing that will be.

Blessings,
Peter.

Biography

Peter McHugh's life has regularly been turned upside down when the Lord has sovereignly interrupted him. These encounters have resulted in profound insights around the love of God and the nature of His Kingdom. He shares these revelations in his books and lives them out. He is a sought-after speaker, mentor, leader and pastor to pastors. He is the founding pastor emeritus of Stairway Church, Melbourne, Australia.

www.ingramcontent.com/pod-product-compliance
Lightning Source LLC
Chambersburg PA
CBHW030551080526
44585CB00012B/341